JOSEPH

SERVE BEHIND THE SCENES TO SET THE STAGE

PHILIP STROUSE

WESTBOW
PRESS®
A DIVISION OF THOMAS NELSON
& ZONDERVAN

This book is a work of non-fiction. Unless otherwise noted, the author
and the publisher make no explicit guarantees as to the accuracy of
the information contained in this book and in some cases, names of
people and places have been altered to protect their privacy.

WestBow Press books may be ordered through booksellers or by contacting:

WestBow Press
A Division of Thomas Nelson & Zondervan
1663 Liberty Drive
Bloomington, IN 47403
www.westbowpress.com
844-714-3454

Scripture taken from the New King James Version® Copyright © 1982
by Thomas Nelson. Used by permission. All rights reserved.

ISBN: 978-1-6642-0657-1 (sc)
ISBN: 978-1-6642-0656-4 (hc)
ISBN: 978-1-6642-0867-4 (e)

Library of Congress Control Number: 2020920111

Print information available on the last page.

WestBow Press rev. date: 10/28/2020

ACKNOWLEDGMENTS

To the WestBow Press team members who patiently worked with me to see this project to completion.

To my wife, the other 50 percent of my being—worthy of Proverbs 31 praise and adoration.

To my two sons, who fill every heartbeat with thankfulness and purpose.

To my brother, who was the foremost editor and thought-polisher in this endeavor.

To my mother, who continues to inspire—who taught me how to walk physically and spiritually.

To my biological father, who provided an innate appreciation for literature and the art of writing.

To my heavenly Father, by whose mercy I haven't received what I deserved and by whose grace I've received what I didn't.

DEDICATION

To every immortal* who spends precious and passing moments on earth reading this book. May the time invested by the author in producing it and the time spent by the reader absorbing it be blessed in propelling people of every tribe and tongue on their predestined paths of divine purpose.

---

* "There are no ordinary people"—from "The Weight of Glory," a C. S. Lewis sermon delivered June 8, 1941.

THIS BOOK WAS FORGED
ON THE EVE OF THE 400ᵀᴴ ANNIVERSARY
OF THE FOUNDING OF THE PLYMOUTH COLONY
AND AT THE THRESHOLD OF THE
250ᵀᴴ ANNIVERSARIES
OF THE VOLLEY ON LEXINGTON GREEN, THE
SKIRMISH AT CONCORD'S NORTH BRIDGE,
AND THE BATTLE OF BUNKER HILL.

CONTENTS

PROLOGUE

One lived more than 3,000 years ago and was a forerunner.
One lived 2,000 years ago and was the Fulfillment.
One lived 250 years ago and was a reflection.

He was the firstborn of Mary and Joseph.

The oldest of several brothers, he was not born into royalty
or the upper class of society, but he became a teacher,
healer, and great orator who inspired hundreds throughout
precincts and even thousands across provinces.

He tended to the physical and emotional needs of the
indigent and outcast while also sitting down to eat and
philosophize with the spiritual and political leaders of
a city besieged by an imposing world empire.

There was a traitor within his closest circle of confidants.

His words and example led disparate people to unite and act.

Soldiers brutally ended his life while others retreated.

He died on a hill outside the city so that others
could live and attain true freedom.

His life served as the catalyst for a movement that
altered human history, reverberated across distant
lands, and changed the world forever.

PREAMBLE

Many Americans know the following names and their exploits in forging a new nation.

Samuel Adams
John Hancock
Paul Revere
George Washington
John Adams
Thomas Jefferson
Benjamin Franklin

These patriots and forefathers of the United States of America brought forth a form and function of government—by the people and for the people—that many around the world still try to grasp and multitudes attempt to emulate. Despite America's past and present imperfections, throngs of immigrants still seek to reach her shores. She is one of just a few countries throughout human history in which fellow citizens would rather cooperate and contend with one another than flee to a preconceived life of better opportunities somewhere else.

There is one name missing from the above list—one who for more than 150 years has been overlooked in prominent annals of American history. His convictions and sacrifice organized and propelled a disparate people's struggle for independence from the British Empire's increasing tyranny and intransigent oppression. That his name is not more prominent in historical discussions and the public consciousness remains an enigma to this day.

While many of the brave and boisterous men of the late eighteenth century contemplated pledging their sacred honor on parchment, he birthed this creed with his own blood. Should he have survived the Battle of Bunker Hill (on Breed's Hill), he would have been a leading nominee and contender for first president of these United States.

His given name and story are eerily similar to those of namesakes from ancient times and distant lands—stories focused on purpose, not prominence or position. On faith instead of fame. On collaboration instead of collusion. On sacrifice and service overcoming sarcasm and strife. His lot is with those whose identities and ideals are discovered behind the scenes in supporting roles so that future generations might have the opportunity to better understand the importance of true unity through the lens of divine liberty.

The full measure of thy life
will not show
until what ye sow begins to grow.

And that which grows begins to show
the path ye went and what was spent.

So spend ye well, for time will tell.

CHAPTER ONE

TEA AND A TIMBER RATTLESNAKE

Boston's North End, Massachusetts Colony | April 18, 1775

It was a night like few others that produced a morning to remember.

THE WANING GIBBOUS MOON SLOWLY RISES IN AN ODD POSITION southeast of Boston on this restless April eve. The Royal Navy's HMS *Somerset*—anchored in the Charles River to block any unauthorized passage to neighboring towns—sits in direct contrast to this celestial anomaly as if in dogged defiance to nature itself. This opposing moon and ship alignment forms a unique corridor through which a well-known Son of Liberty may pass undetected to notify a nascent nation. Lanterns and moonlight, alleyways and shadows—this night will birth a different day.

Under cover of darkness on Boston's North End late that fateful night, Paul Revere boards a strategically moored rowboat pointed toward Charlestown, lying north-northwest across the void. Into the cold water go the muffled oars, slicing silently and steadily through the ink-black depths. He must slip quietly past the seventy-gun British man-of-war while it and prowling longboats try to prevent any colonist's movement after the evening curfew.

Just a few hours before, British soldiers, better known as redcoats, closed the Boston Neck land bridge and Charlestown ferry crossing. Throughout the Massachusetts countryside, more redcoats conduct roving patrols to enforce a lockdown in preparation for the supposed surprise march and raids on Lexington and Concord.

Revere's little skiff, dwarfed by the *Somerset's* massive hull, slides by uncontested under the camouflage of confusing shadows on its determined course. Near the Charlestown shore a furlong or so upriver, attentive patriots—alerted by the posting of two lanterns in the steeple of the Old North Church—carefully saddle a steed for this crucial midnight ride.

Back on the Boston Common, British troops muster to make final preparations before launching their longboats across the same river Revere has just traversed, for a similar yet opposing purpose. The clashes set to occur a few hours later—at Lexington Green, Concord's North Bridge, and Menotomy village—will either unleash the call for liberty or crush it definitively. These are the hours when slumber and indecision are jolted by a call for courage and action.

The midnight ride of Paul Revere, along with that of William Dawes and Samuel Prescott, was not something quickly cobbled together or spontaneously created, as popular culture and poems imply. It was part of an elaborate alert system connected to a web of informants and the original band of brothers, the Sons of Liberty. Its machinations were months in the making, and the musket shots on Lexington Green the morning of April 19, 1775, were packed with the emotional gunpowder of the Boston Massacre five years before and subsequent British intransigencies. Primarily in Boston, but also felt in varying degrees across the other colonies, the increasingly heavy hand of the British government was taking its toll on the loyalty and patience of a burgeoning population.

Boston had seen its share of misery and insults. The smallpox epidemic of 1764,[1] and the constant threat of its resurgence, haunted the inhabitants from all walks of life. It was the pestilence that lurked along cobblestone streets, within the close confines of humble homes, and as the unwanted cargo of arriving ships. Lieutenant Governor Thomas Hutchinson, John and Abigail Adams, and other prominent figures in eastern Massachusetts had their families inoculated against the pox. It was through this plague that the Adamses encountered a physician who later became their dear friend; one with whom they grew extremely close through a more prominent and widespread struggle.

The ships that transported the pox carried other caustic messages and merchandise. Some of the British Parliament's most egregious legislation to tax and regulate the colonies—such as the Sugar, Stamp, and Townshend Acts—were a constant source of insult and inflammation. In 1773, the Tea Act—the only remaining vestige of the 1767 Townshend Acts[2]—set the stage for turning outrage into action. It was a reminder that a remote Parliament could impose taxes at will—the "taxation without representation" infringement that posed a clear and present danger to the Massachusetts Charter and overall function of provincial government across the colonies. It was arbitrary power of the most blatant form wrapped in the packaging of East India Company tea. The major colonial seaports—Boston, New York, Philadelphia, and Charleston—were targeted for compliance.[3] Boston was the first port to receive the tea and thus bore the responsibility as first to respond.

But even the oft-bellicose Boston patriots knew to proceed cautiously with this latest challenge. Their measured process of deliberation and decision making was anchored in previous years' cloistered discussions in a large room—the Long Room—above the *Boston Gazette* print shop,[4] around Liberty Tree on Essex Street,[5] and in the Green Dragon Tavern.[6,7] The *Gazette*'s publishers, Benjamin Edes and John Gill, were sympathetic to the Whig and patriot positions of colonial rights instead of blind deference to the Crown espoused by Tory and loyalist counterparts. This newspaper was the source of many articles and editorials that today are treasured records of our nation's literary DNA. The beloved Liberty Tree was where Bostonians would gather and occasionally hang effigies of detested officials (e.g., stamp masters and tax collectors) as pronouncements of their anger. These places of meeting echo a distant land east of the Mediterranean—where a rugged tree led to liberty, an upper room housed believers about to upend world order, and even a pagan location was used by Christ to declare that the gates of hell would not prevail against a rapidly approaching moment and movement.[8]

More than just a tempest in a teapot

The ominous and ironic first-day-of-the-week moment for the Boston patriots materialized when the tea-laden *Dartmouth* sailed into port on Sunday, November 28, 1773.[9] It was soon joined by two other ships, the *Eleanor* and *Beaver*. The crates of tea were metaphorical barrels of gunpowder, and any spark of emotion or clumsy misstep could ignite a chain reaction of deadly repercussions. Thomas Hutchinson, who had replaced Francis Bernard as the crown-appointed governor, refused to stall the delivery of the tea or return it to England despite many pleas by the citizenry to do so. A deadline was set: the tea would either be landed per British dictate or would have to be consigned to a watery grave. The mere skirmish that precipitated the Boston Massacre of 1770 paled in comparison to what was about to occur through organized action and uncommon resolve.

The patriot leaders met frequently during the first half of December. Still loyal to King George III, although they opposed Parliament's heavy hand, the Sons of Liberty beseeched Governor Hutchinson for assistance in averting a crisis. But just as Moses and Aaron encountered with Pharaoh, sanguine rationale was met with stubborn resistance. Calibrated discussions in the Long Room and at the tree and tavern led to a crescendo on Thursday evening of December 16, 1773. People from miles around gathered at the Old South Meeting House, Boston's southside sister structure of the Old North Church, as it could hold a larger crowd than that of Faneuil Hall—the other prominent public gathering place of colonial Boston. If Boston was the birthplace of the Revolution, then the Old South Meeting House and Faneuil Hall were the cradles. It is interesting to note in today's secular society that the original messages inspiring liberty and illuminating independence emanated from the Old South and Old North churches—entities dedicated to a faith in something more than human eyes can see and mortal minds can frame.

Among the patriot organizers and speakers at the rostrum that December night was Samuel Adams, a leading Son of Liberty with a firebrand style like that of Peter the apostle. He, along with his cousin John Adams, eloquent orator Josiah Quincy, Jr., and close colleague John Hancock, kept the crowd engaged while they awaited word on whether their final appeal to Hutchinson would be granted or denied. They eventually received word that the governor was not interested in the perspective of the populace; the hour had come for the Destruction of the Tea. Samuel Adams gave the cue to those waiting in the wings to proceed as planned. What transpired over the next few hours of that mid-December night was later referred to by historians as "an iconic episode in the creation of the United States"[10] and "in its consequences, proved second only to the Declaration of Independence."[11]

What we now fondly refer to as the Boston Tea Party was a methodical mission of patriots disguised as Mohawk Indians to systematically board the three ships and dump the crates of tea into the harbor. Oversimplification of the event causes us to think a mob of men just donned outfits and ran down to Griffin's Wharf, where unassuming vessels were moored. But the approach to the ships and the hours-long operation required organization, oversight, and timed teamwork. While the Long Room Club leaders Samuel, John, Josiah, and John lingered at Old South, other prominent Sons of Liberty were conspicuously absent from the proceedings.

Given the dire ramifications if something went awry with such a bold act against British property and principle, there needed to be a trusted, on-scene orchestrator to coordinate all the movements.[12] One usually prominent speaker and instigator was missing from the visible faces at the Old South gathering—the same one who later played the supporting role behind Paul's midnight ride and inoculated John Adams's family from the dreaded smallpox. He gave voice to the lifeless following the 1770 Boston Massacre and was this night the most probable caller of cadence and composure along the waterfront.[13]

The stakes couldn't have been greater, for an unconstrained mob mentality would bring about a series of negative consequences that their larger aims would not survive. A resolute yet surgical response was required to confront this forced importation of tea—a calculated act of arbitrary power by the British Empire. It represented the "passage of an American Rubicon"[14]—the point of no return: a revolutionary act against the mother country's capricious mandates. If the other colonies perceived the Boston group as overreacting and instigating a premature revolt to British rule, they would quickly distance themselves from this band of brigands.

Unity: the prime commodity

Therefore, unity was the prime commodity that the patriots needed to develop and sustain, not squander, as Boston couldn't proceed down this path alone. It would need the support and solidarity of neighboring towns and the strength of sister colonies. Building unity within and without was paramount as the city already was fragmented into factions of Whigs and patriots versus Tories and loyalists. In aiming for greater consensus and collaboration, the Boston Whigs created a Committee of Correspondence in 1772,[15] the year before the Tea Party, to institute a means of sharing ideas and updates with other communities and like-minded colonial groups.

Almost as if a practice run for the popular midnight ride, the Committee of Correspondence promptly dispatched Paul Revere like a pony express rider to deliver news about the Destruction of the Tea to New York and Philadelphia. The committee also sent letters about the evolving situation to Benjamin Franklin and Arthur Lee, who were in England on behalf of the colonies.[16] As 1773 gave way to the dawning of a new year, so too did the paradigm shift from subservience under remote royalty into the larger struggle for liberty.

The full pursuit for freedom from the reigning world empire would require colonial harmony and determination. Words would need to transform into action. And while the pen is indeed mightier than the sword, the quill's tenor and timing must partner with the blade in dictating which direction it should point and the manner of force with which it should swing. The committee's creation and correspondence with sister colonies brought a smile to the face of Franklin. A coiled snake is nothing to meddle with when cornered.

When a serpent was sublime instead of subtle

In 1751—more than twenty years before the Destruction of the Tea— Benjamin Franklin wrote a satirical commentary in the *Pennsylvania Gazette* suggesting that as a way to thank the British government for its policy of sending convicted felons to America, the colonists should send rattlesnakes to England.[17] The basis of his thought was that the British brethren on the royal isle should feel the painful and poisonous ramifications of their disregard for their fellow countrymen across the Atlantic. While Franklin's attention in the 1750s shifted to the threat of the French on the western frontier, he reverted to pointing the fangs at Britain in the 1770s when her boots began trampling the very villages and woodlands she previously had defended.

The symbology of the serpentine metaphor grew exponentially in 1754 when Franklin created the colonies' first political cartoon,[18] which showed a snake in several pieces—each segment representing a portion of the colonies—with the bold phrase, "Join, or Die." It was intended to emphasize the importance of colonial unity during the French and Indian War.

THE IMAGE AS IT APPEARED IN THE *PENNSYLVANIA GAZETTE* OF MAY 9, 1754.
SOURCE: LIBRARY OF CONGRESS.[19]

Franklin used it to visualize the need when he met with other representatives in Albany, New York, that May in proffering the idea of forming a unified government by which the colonies could collaborate in matters of defense. His grand vision—a unified group of delegates representing all the colonies—was twenty-two years ahead of schedule. Provincial jealousies, human suspicion, and obstructionist politics got in the way.

While there are more appealing aspects of nature to represent a people—a lion, a winged raptor, or another majestic beast—Franklin chose the snake. He did so due to its demeanor of not seeking out confrontation but also not shrinking from self-defense when provoked. It delivers a pinpoint yet lethal blow against any aggressor after first providing ample warning through its numerous rattles (colonies) moving in unison that it should neither be trifled with nor trampled on. The imagery inspired the bright yellow Gadsden Flag and Navy Jack with their unmistakable "Don't Tread on Me" snakes and statements of resolve—resolve that was called upon in Boston in 1774–1775 when British boots trampled cobblestone streets and countryside crossings.

Following the December 1773 Destruction of the Tea, the inhabitants of Boston prepared for the eventual and heavy-handed response by the British forces who had once defended them from foreign threats just a few years ago. The patriots' action would be met with overwhelming reaction, intended to intimidate, punish, and send a message to the rest of the colonies.

During this period of dread and uncertainty, a song about liberty[20] provided solace and singleness of purpose toward a grand endeavor yet to be fully understood. It ended with the phrase "for brave America!" in similar fashion to a poem Francis Scott Key penned forty years later (in 1814) that became the national anthem. This earlier song roused kinship and bolstered the determination of a people about to go through their darkest days in pursuit of the brightest of lights. Its most likely author was that Son of Liberty who—from behind the scenes—was inoculating, coordinating, orchestrating, and dispatching. Progress in a worthy purpose is best achieved when the major players aren't clamoring for name recognition and sole ownership of the credit.

The winter and spring anticipation of reaction turned into reality when General Thomas Gage, the commander of all British forces in North America, arrived in May 1774 as the newly-appointed governor general of Massachusetts.[21] In 1773, British ships brought tea. In 1774, they brought another egregious shipment of British troops.

British military operations were based out of Castle William, the military fortification on a strategic island southeast of Boston.[22] Its separation yet proximity to the city led to its dual use as a smallpox hospital during the 1764 epidemic and continuously occupied military installation from which to plan, stage, and launch operations.[23] The British troops withdrew to this location following the Boston Massacre in March 1770,[24] and it served the same purpose as did the Antonia Fortress in Jerusalem for Pontius Pilate and his garrison of Roman soldiers—a place to house a large contingent of military forces to keep a restless population in check.

As armed confrontation became a reality in mid-April 1775, the timing of bloodshed couldn't have been more momentous. It coincided with the week of Passover and Unleavened Bread. These were the sacred events and remembrances initiated thousands of years ago during Moses's confrontations with an Egyptian Pharaoh and fulfilled with Jesus's unwavering stance before the Sanhedrin, Pilate, Herod, and the people He was dying to save. Similar focus and resolve were about to be displayed in eighteenth century New England at Lexington and Concord.

In the tense hours of darkness shortly before that first "shot heard around the world," the world's foremost military of British boats and troops scoured the water and roads for any unauthorized movement. Which prompts the question: How is it they missed Paul Revere rowing across the Charles River from Boston to Charlestown, the epicenter of all the activity?

- 9 -

The enigma hinges on the celestial anomaly of the moon's irregular position on the night of April 18, 1775.[25,26] Occurring shortly after that year's Passover, which always occurs at full moon per the Hebrew calendar, the moon's placement and brightness provide the clue.

In its subsequent waning gibbous phase, the moon illuminated objects small and great transiting the river. But the odd angle of its orbit that year meant it cast a curtain of long shadows as it slowly rose from behind the Boston cityscape. Instead of serving as a floodlight from a more easterly moonrise location as was the norm, it was like a high-beam headlight shining directly at the raised platforms on the British men-of-war. From a sentry's point of view scanning the surface of the water from the deck of the *Somerset*, the nearly-horizontal moonlight during Revere's transit would have saturated the soldier's eyes, drastically reducing his night vision when trying to look down and out across the water.

By the time Revere was on the other shore and settling into stirrups and saddle, the moon had risen to a more prominent position of illuminator instead of concealer. The road and villages lying on Revere's westerly track were soon awash in light as if on cue.

The dichotomy of concealment by darkness and direction by light

It was as if Exodus 14:20 was again set in motion whereby the pillar of cloud and fire separated the fleeing Israelites from the pursuing Egyptians, giving light to one side while bestowing darkness to the other. Again, both occurrences were in the days immediately following the Passover—first for a people fleeing Egyptian bondage, and then for a people seeking release from British oppression.

Thus, the moon played a supporting role often overlooked in setting the stage for a dramatic act of historical renown. Even with five lunar references in Henry Wadsworth Longfellow's poem *Paul Revere's Ride*,[27] the moon takes a back seat to the two points of light from the dual lanterns serving as signals in the Old North Church steeple.

———•———

And just as the waning gibbous moon played a largely overlooked
yet crucial supporting role in Revere's ride,
so too did a prominent physician and public servant named Joseph.

———•———

Dr. Joseph Warren (June 1741–June 1775) *concealed* the movements
of the Boston Tea Party and activated the alarm system that produced
Revere's midnight mission. He *illuminated* the need for unity of effort
through his various roles on committees and numerous writings plus
prime-time speeches commemorating the Boston Massacre. And he was
a catalyst for the colonial unity and the joint mind-set that Franklin
envisioned and animated.

Even though he was a person of prominent position in Boston,
Dr. Warren elected to stand in the same trenches of the Breed's Hill
redoubt as his neighbors of lower rank and meager means. His final act
of standing in the gap on June 17, 1775, galvanized a people and set the
stage for the recently commissioned General George Washington and a
newly created Continental Army that stood near that hallowed soil just
a few weeks later. His life and the willful giving of it inspired Thomas
Jefferson's pen strokes at the Graff House on Philadelphia's Market
Street as a bold declaration of independence began to materialize the
following year.

Dr. Warren's given name was more than a mere coincidence when
one considers the major forebears of this designation. Though the
name Joseph could be considered common, especially in Puritan New
England, the actions of the namesakes described in these pages are quite
the contrary. They are dedicated to causes greater than themselves with
a patience and persistence that sustained them in their supporting roles.
It's not about being at the forefront for recognition's sake, but standing
in the gap and shouldering the load so that the mission moves forward.
It's about becoming a servant-leader, living by example, and fulfilling
your life's purpose by seeing it from Someone else's perspective.

Burn the ships and smash the oars;
pivot thine anger to His Majesty's shores.

Or pause with wisdom and contemplate
a better fate through a different gate.

Where patient planning
and preparation
lead to actions that birth a nation.

'Tis no small matter or ease of force
to tame the challenge and stay the course.

There's much to do, this task of ours
on a night of shadows and distant stars.

CHAPTER TWO

MORE THAN TWO TAKE THE SHIP

East of Eden, pre-Mesopotamia | ~ 2,348 BC[1] | Genesis 6–9

Science and a ship; destruction, dispersion, and dispensations.

THROUGHOUT HISTORY, THERE HAVE BEEN NOTABLE EVENTS connected to ships and their contents, context, and consequences—the *Santa Maria, Mayflower*, HMS *Victory, La Amistad*, RMS *Titanic*, RMS *Lusitania*, USS *Arizona*, USS *Missouri*, and the list goes on. Without question, the most epic instance produced an almost unfathomable reset of life throughout the planet. It was so great that it is reflected in separate yet similar stories across ancient cultures. The biblical account of Noah's flood seems too big to believe and too catastrophic to have occurred. But an open-minded look at recent research and objective science within and across a variety of disciplines—geology, paleontology, biology, zoology, and meteorology—provide the telltale signs of a global deluge. The point here is not to describe all the evidence and ramifications of this massive event but to consider two Joseph-related aspects that presage other epic events in both the Levant and the Western Hemisphere.

The first aspect is a closer look at Noah's third-mentioned son, Japheth. His name in Hebrew means "expansion"[2] or "to enlarge" and is an antediluvian version of the name Yosef or Joseph, which means "let him add"[3] or "he shall increase"[4] in the form of exponential multiplication, unfolding, and magnification. Genesis 9:18–19 is clear that Noah's three sons (Shem, Ham, and Japheth) are the ancestors of all humans after the Great Flood, and thus this passage also dispels the notion that the event was just a regional anomaly related to a Black Sea or Caspian Sea catastrophe as secular theories postulate.

> *These three were the sons of Noah, and from*
> *these the whole earth was populated.*[5]

Genesis 10:2 and 1 Chronicles 1:5 show that Japheth had seven sons. Many historical references describe him as the father of the Indo-European nations and the progenitor of the people and tribes that also migrated to Russia, throughout Asia, across Siberia, and into the Americas via the Bering Strait. It is interesting to note that while Japheth's name usually follows those of his brothers, Shem and Ham, in scripture; Genesis 10 and 1 Chronicles 1 both begin with his genealogy.

Several of his sons' names (Gomer, Magog, Tubal, and Meshech) reappear in the books of Ezekiel and Revelation, as their descendants figure prominently in prophetic events. As witnessed in just the past century of human history, Japheth's offspring are capable of creating great technological advancements for society while also being culpable in releasing horrendous atrocities (e.g., Auschwitz and atomic weapons). The expansion, enlargement, and exponential connotations related to the names Japheth and Joseph can have the effect of a double-edged sword for humanity, depending on how it's wielded.

The second aspect builds upon the number seven as reflected in Japheth's genealogy and rapid expansion across the globe. In a quick and casual reading of the Genesis account of preparing for the Flood, many people imagine two massive elephants, two full-grown lions, two tigers, two towering giraffes—two of every animal known to modern zoology before recent extinctions. A closer look at Genesis 6:19–20 shows that a representative *kind* or *sort* of each animal, akin to the level of either *family* or *genus* in today's taxonomy terms,[6] was the defining point of delineation for containing the requisite DNA capable of producing the hundreds of thousands of species in subsequent millennia. And the ark, with dimensions similar to a modern cargo ship, had quite the carrying capacity.[7] Recent analysis, using conservative calculations, describes its volume as approximately 1.5 million cubic feet of space, equivalent to more than 550 railroad boxcars.[8]

But Genesis 7 is where the story really unfolds when considering exponential capability. In Genesis 6, Noah was to take two of each animal, a male and a female. In Genesis 7, there's an additional stipulation pertaining to clean animals and creatures that fly. Many in religious circles focus on just the "seven" and "clean" and assume the passage is referring to simply seven of each clean type of animal, with the seventh or odd-numbered animal being for sacrificial purposes. However, Genesis 7:2–3, through the lens of the Hebrew language, is describing seven pairs—seven males and seven females—when mentioning the clean creatures and every sort that takes to the air.[9] The details of Genesis 6 and 7 don't contradict one another; in fact, the two passages complement and clarify the equation that verses 6:19–20 emphasize, which is that there were two—a couple/pair—of each animal. Therefore, the constant in the equation is already established for verses 7:2–3, so the insertion of seven of each kind really means fourteen. The focus wasn't on two as the total but on the pairing aspect—the unity of a male and female—to be seen as a joined entity, one of the most basic yet beautiful examples of unity: unity that ultimately produces new life—the pro*create* aspect of miracles. Neither partner is subordinate to the other, but all of the potential strengths and abilities of each entity, when combined, truly exemplify Aristotle's axiom that "the whole is greater than the sum of its parts." The ark—surrounded by a watery world of cataclysmic upheaval and destruction—was a floating capsule of explosive potential for new and abundant life.

Therefore, while at least two of every unclean land-based beast and creeping thing boarded the boat, there were fourteen of every clean animal and *fourteen* of each kind of flying fowl. It was like a reset to the fifth day of Creation (Genesis 1:20–23) when the waters and the air were the two domains teeming with life to prepare the new environment for the sixth day.

When released after the Flood, birds would go forth to disperse and fertilize plant seeds across virgin continents and remote isles—developing new ecosystems in advance of the lumbering herds and the predators that pursued them in packs and prides. The coastlines could not contain them, and mountains would not restrict their movements. The canyons and vales were but glideslopes for them, and stalwart trees became their perches of grand panoramas. And their curtain call all began with the release of a ravenous raven and a determined dove.

———•———

Genesis 8 gives the timing of the floodwaters' receding and Noah's gauging of the situation through these two birds. The raven was released and didn't return to the sole sanctuary on the water, but it floats upon the surface debris and feasts upon the decaying flesh, signifying the massive destruction. It hearkens back to the situation of Genesis 1:2 when "the earth was without form, and void; and darkness was on the face of the deep. And the Spirit of God was hovering over the face of the waters." The raven preyed upon the carnage of death and was cloaked in darkness, not wanting to return to the one it came from. The dove, representing the Spirit (see Matthew 3:16; Mark 1:10; Luke 3:22; John 1:32), flew over the same watery realm that the raven claimed as his habitation.

The dove's mission was to gauge the ground situation, and she performed this flight pattern on a seven-day schedule—signifying the various dispensations of how the Spirit would interact with humankind. On her first flight, the dove found no place to rest, for everything was tainted by death—the dispensation from Adam to Moses (Romans 5:14). On her second flight, the dove spent the majority of the day traversing the landscape, returning in the evening with an olive leaf, the initial sign of peace, symbolizing the dispensation from Moses to John the Baptist (Luke 16:16). This epoch was characterized by the law of blood sacrifices to assuage the judgment of sin, the prophets giving instruction and admonition, and the temporary alighting of the Spirit upon humans (see Judges 13:24–25; 1 Chronicles 12:18; 1 Samuel 10:10). On her third and final flight, the dove didn't return after spending a few hours moving through the atmosphere but remained on the earth. The Spirit now abides in humans instead of just resting upon them in the current dispensation of grace (the book of Acts and subsequent epistles). "Noah removed the covering" (Genesis 8:13), and "the veil of the temple was torn in two" (Matthew 27:51; Mark 15:38; Luke 23:45).

Boston Harbor, Massachusetts Colony | December 16, 1773
Unsweet iced tea.

And so, in this waning dispensation of grace, darkness covers the face of the waters across a quiet Boston Harbor on a cold December night. Being the most active and important British port in the New World at that time, it serves as the gateway to the vast expanse of flora and fauna in a theater containing thirteen colonies and hundreds of indigenous tribes. At the edge of this arena, the stage is set with three boats about to be boarded for the epic event described in the previous chapter. The British rulers will not return the tea to England, and the colonists refuse to pay the tax that will be imposed if the cargo is unloaded. The only option is destruction of the crates without doing damage to the ships or any other property or person. Even a perfectly executed plan will have dire consequences for any of those identified as participating in this rebellious act against Parliament's mandate. Thus, a disguise is needed.

Many historical accounts specifically describe the raiders' concealment as Mohawk markings and other unique attributes of this particular tribe. The Sons of Liberty weren't careless or indiscriminate in the selection of their camouflage—they valued symbolism and carefully chose the distinct apparel for this main act on center stage. They didn't pick Native American garb in flippant mockery or so that any indigenous people would be blamed—quite the contrary. Using these specific outfits was a sign of respect and admiration—a uniform meant to send a larger message than just defiance against a tax.

The Mohawk homeland wasn't near the Boston area, as that was the realm of the Wampanoag, Massachusett, and Nauset peoples—the inhabitants of the Dawnland, the place of first light from the rising sun.[10] Rather, the Mohawks lived among the picturesque lakes and woodlands of what is now northeastern New York State and western Vermont. They were part of a renowned six-nation Haudenosaunee Confederacy,[11] what the Europeans referred to as the Iroquois League.[12] They traded with the Dutch in the 1600s and were allied with the English throughout the 1700s; their skill and bravery were vital to the British victory in the French and Indian War (1754–1763).

Recall that in May 1754, Benjamin Franklin and other delegates from the various colonies met in Albany, New York, to discuss matters of unity and common defense against their French and allied adversaries. It's not mere coincidence that Albany sat at the doorstep of the great Mohawk people and the larger Iroquois League. The Haudenosaunee model of peace, cooperation, and mutual defense among the various tribes, with agreements that maintained tribal and individual liberties, was studied and highly regarded by Franklin and the other Founders. While the tea tax represented tyranny, the Mohawk represented autonomy, unified strength, and an indigenous icon in alliance with the Crown.

Within the Haudenosaunee Confederacy, the Mohawks were "the keepers of the eastern door,"[13] given their easternmost location among that league of nations. And through that door of engagement with the colonists, Benjamin Franklin and others who figured prominently in shaping the Declaration of Independence and framing the U.S. Constitution were inspired by the Haudenosaunee ideals of liberty, the consent of the governed, and the council of representatives drawn from all of the tribes' clans. Moreover, the Iroquois League's Great Law of Peace,[14] like the Magna Carta, served as an enlightening example of ideas from which to establish a nation.

———•———

An eagle and arrows – strength through unity, *e pluribus unum*.

———•———

The Mohawk people and the other tribes developed their confederacy after coming to the realization that a single arrow is easily snapped while a bundle of arrows is nearly impossible to break. From this understanding came the symbolism of an eagle's clutch of arrows representing each tribe bound together with others for a stronger common defense. On the Great Seal of the United States, found on the back of every dollar bill, the eagle holds thirteen arrows in its left talons, representing the unified defense of the original thirteen colonies. And in the right talons is an olive branch, like that of Noah's determined dove.

The Sons of Liberty chose the Mohawk disguise to symbolize unity and determination, continued allegiance to the Crown despite the trying circumstances, individual liberty coupled with cooperation, and the Massachusetts patriots as the keepers of the eastern door for the rest of their soon-to-be-confederated colonies. These New England protagonists stood up to the challenge on the northeastern flank of this tyrannical tea tax, and how they held the line or broke ranks would resonate throughout the Eastern Seaboard.

They carefully destroyed the tea in 1773 without taking up arms or degenerating into mass riots against the local British troops. The group of disguised men moved quietly in organized fashion onto the boats in like manner and cadence to what Noah would have witnessed millennia ago. These Sons of Liberty continued to focus on the olive branch of peace and reconciliation until the situation required the sharpness of arrows in 1775.

Both in the Boston Tea Party operation of December 1773 and the Lexington/Concord alarm of April 1775, Joseph Warren was integral to their planning and execution. In the most ironic sense, his name is not mentioned with the same frequency in American parlance as the other Founders, and yet on the one occasion when his name shouldn't come up, it does. In the clandestine operation of destroying the tea, the Mohawk disguises were meant to send a symbolic message while protecting the identities of those involved.

Whether due to careless exuberance by his countrymen or their felt need that he should receive proper credit, a song wafted down cobblestone streets and throughout taverns in the days following that brisk December night when crates of tea met their ruin. A stanza in the middle of the melody cemented Joseph's name in history in confronting oppression for a greater cause.

> *Our Warren's here, and bold Revere*
> *With hands to do and words to cheer,*
> *for liberty and laws.*[15]

She watches and waits
for her beloved to turn his head.

May she catch his eye for once,
instead of drinking the cup of dread.

When outlook overcomes environment,
and determination supersedes the pain.

She one day awakens to victory,
and a life no longer lived in vain.

But it's a choice that produces a change,
and a spark that creates a flame.

A life initially lived in obscurity
that led to the greatest of fame.

CHAPTER THREE

THE SECRET OF A SUPPORTING ROLE

Haran, the Padan-aram region of Upper Mesopotamia
(present-day Turkey, near the Syrian border)
~ 1760 BC[1] | Genesis 29

Contentment overcomes jealousy.

BEFORE THERE WAS A SON OF JACOB NAMED JOSEPH—THE firstborn son of the patriarch's cherished wife Rachel—there was an overlooked and underappreciated Leah. As Rachel's older sister, Leah was used as a pawn by her father Laban in a cruel bait-and-switch scheme to ensnare Jacob into nearly another decade of servitude for a spouse. The original agreement was that Jacob would work for Laban seven years so that Rachel could become his wife. The morning after their wedding consummation, Jacob realized he had been joined to the less appealing Leah rather than to the one his heart desired.

The arrangement not only shook Jacob's plans in a drastic way, but it also dramatically altered the remainder of Leah's life on earth. She was instantly thrust into being the unwanted wife of a husband she yearned to please, to impress, and to fully connect with in the most intimate way. Not only did she lack Rachel's beautiful appearance, but Jacob likely perceived Leah to be an extra burden, another mouth to feed, an additional person in the way. Overall, Jacob viewed Leah with contempt rather than affection, as she was the constant reminder of his being hoodwinked by his father-in-law.

———•———

It was the epitome of the supplanter being supplanted—poetic justice for how Jacob had fooled his father, Isaac, into thinking he was someone else for the sake of personal gain.[2]

———•———

Thus, Jacob received the rotten end of the firstborn protocol, the dichotomy of his desire and disdain, when Laban informed him that Leah, as the older sister, had to be given away first. Her father didn't want her, and her husband didn't either.

Here was the tragedy of feeling unwanted, both as a child and as a spouse, all wrapped into one situation.

———•———

But despite her outward appearance and emotionally debilitating circumstances, Leah possessed a unique inner beauty of strength and determination. Instead of sulking in a tent away from the rest of the family for the rest of her life, Leah set her mind at capturing her husband's love. She pursued it by trying to immerse herself in the wife's cultural role of that day—producing children, especially sons.

Over the course of many years, enduring grueling competition, Leah bore Jacob six of his twelve sons while the other three women in the household, Rachel and their respective handmaids-turned-concubines, each bore him two. In quickly doing the math, Leah enjoyed more than the double-portion blessing, which would have equated to bearing *four* male heirs for the man she was trying to please, not the even more impressive *six* strapping sons. The first three—Reuben, Simeon, and Levi—possessed names that echoed Leah's early attempts to gain Jacob's attention in that they meant, respectively, "see/behold a son – see me, notice me," "hearing – hear me, listen to me," and "attached – join me, be with me."[3,4] Leah's insatiable intent throughout the first half of her childbearing phase of life was to be noticed, to become the center of attention—the apple of her husband's eye. She was following the same pattern of using her children as bartering pieces as her father Laban had done with her.

But by the time Leah had born her fourth son, her focus matured and pivoted from an earthly and egotistical realm to a heavenly and holistic one. She named this fourth son Judah, meaning "celebrate, praise [Jehovah]."[5,6] Leah's paradigm shifted from *receiving* attention and adoration to *giving* it—and giving it to an Entity she couldn't see with human eyes or understand through mortal rationale. Her motivation in life was no longer driven by human acceptance; it had become firmly established in the El or God whom her husband spoke of and to whom he sacrificed. Leah gained an unshakable sense of peace and understanding of ultimate purpose when she realized that her value and true meaning rested in the perspective of the Almighty rather than in fickle and fleeting human emotions.

Become obsessed with the things that matter, and desire that which is truly important and meaningful, not for the moment, but for their worth on the scale of eternal weights and measures.

It's ironic in retrospect to see the spiritual transformation of Rachel and Leah as the story unfolds. Rachel, initially the recipient of Jacob's attention and affection, stole her father's idols when Jacob and his family left Haran for Canaan. Her actions ran contrary to what her grandfather-in-law Abraham had done when he left family and comfortable surroundings for a higher calling. When Laban caught up with Jacob's caravan and searched the tents and animals for the stolen artifacts, Rachel didn't get off the saddle where she had hidden them, claiming she was physically unable to do so.[7] One wonders if the consequences of her unethical actions contributed to her real reproductive system complications in that she died while giving birth to her younger son, whom she named Ben-Oni, meaning "son of my sorrow."[8] Jacob buried her in Bethlehem, which later became known as the first City of David (one of Leah's royal offspring).

Meanwhile, Leah went from a state of barrenness to suckling the sons from whom Moses, David, and the eventual Messiah would come. She bore Levi upon her lap, the patriarch of Moses the deliverer and lawgiver plus the entire lineage of his brother Aaron and the Levitical priesthood. Bringing forth Judah, she was the mother of the Davidic dynasty that later reigned supreme over ancient Israel and one day will be established without end—the quintessential Game of Thrones finale. While Bethlehem represented the end of life for the leading role of Rachel, it epitomizes the beginning of life for the supporting role of Leah. It's the birthplace of both a shepherd boy and the Good Shepherd, who through servanthood and supporting roles in significant portions of their lives, become the ultimate kings.

Leah grew to comprehend the meaning and importance of a supporting rather than a leading role—and she became the matriarch of the Messiah.

When considering death and burial, Leah's final resting place was one of victory and fulfillment. Jacob buried Leah in the cave of Machpelah near Mamre[9] (in present day Hebron), where Abraham placed Sarah and later joined her and where Isaac and Rebekah were laid to rest. With his beloved wife Rachel lying alone in Bethlehem and Leah in the cave of his fathers, Jacob eventually had to decide the place of his own final interment. His conclusion is extraordinary for two reasons—the relative distance factor and the relationship statement.

First, relative distance. Jacob's last years were not spent in Canaan but in Egypt due to the famine that his son Joseph had foreseen, hence saving hundreds of thousands from starvation. If Jacob had been living in Canaan, probably orbiting the Mamre location in his waning years as his father and grandfather had done, it's conceivable he would have simply opted for the Machpelah cave, as it was nearby, whereas Rachel's body was lying more than fourteen miles or twenty-two kilometers to the northeast across the rugged Judean terrain. But from Egypt, hundreds of miles from both burial sites, fourteen miles between the two choices wasn't much of a factor in the transit equation given the relative distances. Thus, it was the second factor of the final resting place decision that carried the most weight in tipping the scales.

With all his sons, representing the twelve tribes of Israel, gathered at his side in life's final moments, Jacob carefully and emphatically issues the command of where he is to be buried, and why. The first two verses of Genesis 49:29–31 describe the place and historical rendering of how Abraham came to possess the plot of ground. But the third verse, verse 31, contains three simple yet strong phrases about the close-knit relationship of husband and wife, which together build to a climax on the last word, *Leah*.

With his few expiring breaths, Jacob emphasizes the relationship statement. He remarked that Sarah was lying there as the wife of Abraham, and that Rebekah was lying there as the wife of Isaac, so Leah was lying there for the same reason. Somehow, she had become the primary wife, occupying a prominent position for Jacob. And with Jacob's God-given name change to Israel—meaning "he will rule as God, having princely power with God"[10]—Leah had become an esteemed princess in an eternal kingdom. In Leah's life of letting go and focusing on the supporting role of offering praise and worship, she gained more than she could have ever imagined, for fairy tales fall short of the final acclaim she received.

In hearkening back to the beginning of Genesis, Sarah was there because she was the bone of Abraham's bones and the flesh of his flesh, as was Rebekah to Isaac, and as Leah became to Jacob. The beloved rib bone that became fused to his side and protected his heart. The bone who learned to serve in a supporting role instead of clamoring for prime position, but who achieved just that by lying next to Jacob every night uncontested for the past 3,700 years.

Points to ponder –

1. Saul, the first king of Israel, was of Rachel's offspring through the tribe of Benjamin. He stood head and shoulders in stature above his countrymen, and his heart became filled with envy and strife in trying to gain more power and adoration for himself. He died a tragic death and lost his lineage grip on the kingdom.
2. David, the second king, was Leah's descendant through Judah. He was just a shepherd boy at the time of his anointing. He endeavored in his heart to pursue after God's heart through poems, songs, and service, even in the sovereign realm. He passed peacefully into eternity with an everlasting reign firmly established.

Perhaps it was Leah's final outlook and heart
condition that formed the foundation
of her many-times-great-grandson David's penitent
and purposeful heart toward God.

The sands of time remain sublime
in a land of enchanted tales.

A young man's dreams came true, it seems,
to tip the largest of scales.

Chapter Four

EGYPT AND A DREAMER

Dothan, Land of Canaan | ~ 1729 BC[1] | Genesis 37

*When a pit, Potiphar's house, and prison are
really preparation for the palace.*

———•———

The Joseph of Genesis – the Joseph of Beginnings

———•———

JOSEPH, THE FAVORED SON OF JACOB, DIDN'T REALIZE THE SILENT chill of the pit until the shock began to wear off after several minutes. Stripped of the colorful outer garment that was a prized possession from his father, Joseph felt the darkness wash over him in a new wave of dread as he tried to wrap his mind around what his brothers had just done. Handled roughly in an act of betrayal, he wondered what the next few moments would hold. He knew they disliked how their father treated him differently and that his retelling of dreams irritated them. But did it justify this? Would they come to their senses and pull him back up to the surface?

After what seemed like hours of waiting and soul-searching, the end of a rope lands on the floor in front of him. Thankful that his brothers have reconsidered their actions, Joseph holds on as they pull him to the top and into the blinding brightness of midday. But then former dread metastasizes into fear as he finds himself standing next to a group of Ishmaelites who are giving twenty pieces of silver to his brothers. His hands are roughly bound as he's secured to one of the camels in the caravan and trudges down the Via Maris (the Way of the Sea) to Egypt. This morning, he woke up as a favored son of promise; this evening, he is a helpless piece of property.

Over the next fourteen or so years, Joseph is transformed from a self-centered teenage dreamer in his father's tent to a humble interpreter of dreams in Pharaoh's throne room. Finding himself in a foreign land, Joseph undergoes a testing period and maturation process that reveal a level of favor much higher than what Jacob could bestow. When an eternal King is pleased with your performance, the notice and acknowledgment of a temporary Pharaoh is sure to follow.

But it requires a journey—not one of geographical distance but of the wider span and deeper depths of a servant's soul in the making. After experiencing two prophetic dreams as a young man, Joseph knew he was destined for great things; he just didn't realize the path of preparation he would have to take to get there. He had to learn it wasn't about colorful coats, bowing sheaves and stars, or a tent full of servants; it was about rags to wash feet, prisoners to lift up and encourage, and *becoming* the attentive servant. Terribly slow and consistent testing over time purges the soul just as a refiner's fire purifies silver.

When Joseph first arrives in Egypt, the Ishmaelite traders sell him to Potiphar, a high-ranking officer in Pharaoh's guard. Joseph fulfills whatever duties are assigned to him and, through faithfulness and favor, progresses to the point of overseeing all the operations of Potiphar's house. But the maturation process isn't a straight-line trajectory of promotion and success.

Through no fault of his own, Joseph again finds himself in the midst of a pit, the high-profile prison known to be the most dreaded dungeon of the realm. His temporary status of liberty was stripped from him because he didn't give in to the sexual advances of his master's wife. Genesis 39:20 states that Joseph was put "into the prison, a place where the king's prisoners were confined." In Joseph's specific situation, it could read, "a place where *the* King's servant was held waiting in the wings."

———•———

Dreams might lead to a dungeon, but prison can lead to a palace.

———•———

A paradox in human interactions is that a person who grasps the importance of a servant's role is usually the one who gets promoted. Joseph went from slave status to Potiphar's assistant and eventually second only to Pharaoh, the greatest of supporting roles in ancient empires. The same could be said for Daniel, Mordecai, and Nehemiah. Those who do well in their relegated roles tend to be elevated by the One who is always in the leading role.

Everything began to improve in rapid fashion for Joseph when he displayed unique wisdom and understanding by being the only one able to interpret Pharaoh's two troubling dreams. And by interpreting others' dreams—the butler's, the baker's, and ultimately Pharaoh's—his own two dreams of promise began to materialize. When the focus shifts from self to service, blessings and fulfillment are released back to the giver in exponential ways.

Pharaoh placed Joseph in command of operations over the entire kingdom and gave him a beautiful wife named Asenath, the daughter of Poti-Pherah, priest of On. The name Poti-Pherah or Potipherah carries the same Egyptian meaning as Potiphar. While this was a different person than his former master, Joseph was blessed with legitimate female companionship from a Potiphar-linked source because he didn't succumb to an illicit relationship with a previous Potiphar-related woman, the original desperate housewife.

And while Joseph was blessed with Asenath, Asenath was blessed in becoming a major part of Hebrew history. She, like Tamar, Rahab, and Ruth—three Gentile women prominently mentioned in Jesus's genealogy (Matthew 1)—came from a pagan background and thus display one of the greatest redemptive allegories related to the bride of Christ. Joseph and Asenath had two sons, Manasseh and Ephraim, who would become the heads of two of Israel's twelve tribes. It didn't matter what Asenath's past had been; her new life and role made her a part of something much bigger. The significance of the story doesn't rest with the temporal positions in a pit, prison, or palace; how the story ends and what it means for subsequent generations is what matters most.

In fulfillment of Pharaoh's dreams, the seven years of plenty give way to seven years of famine. In partial fulfillment of Joseph's dreams, his brothers begin their journey to Egypt—probably on the same Via Maris he had traveled years before—unknowingly to seek help and bow down to the sibling they sold for silver. When they come into Joseph's presence, they don't recognize him due to the foreign setting and his Egyptian appearance. The interactions and testing that transpire over the next several months finally result in a joyous family reunion of all brothers plus their father, Jacob (Israel). This too is an allegory of what will soon take place in world events between the nation of Israel and its Messiah.

These allegories are connected to a larger construct of types and shadows that many rabbis and Bible scholars summarize as Joseph/ Yosef being a foreshadow of Jesus/Yeshuah.[2] He was despised by his brothers, betrayed and sold for pieces of silver, at a young age knew supernatural things (Joseph's dreams | Jesus teaching in the temple at age twelve), arose from captivity to right-hand status of authority, saved Gentile nations, and was again reunited with his people to save them from destruction. Joseph, the son of Rachel, suffered undeserved affliction in order to save others. Jesus, in His first coming to earth, passed through the matrix at Bethlehem where the sacrificial lambs are born. His initial years were connected to Rachel and sorrow as Herod exterminated all the infant boys in the area (Matthew 2:18). He came in the supporting role of a suffering Messiah (*Mashiach ben Yosef*), One who stooped down to wash others' feet, the sacrificial Lamb for each and every human soul.

———•———

While Joseph's name was known far and wide to his contemporaries, it began to fade under the shifting Egyptian sands as time progressed. This is due, ironically, to his position and blessing. First, upon Joseph's promotion as Pharaoh's vizier, his name was changed to Zaphnath-Paaneah.[3] Many speculate on the exact meaning, with the general consensus being that it labels him a revealer of secrets or one who brings forth the mysteries of God to preserve life. Some believe the name Imhotep, a prominent official under Pharaoh Djoser who is described as dealing with a seven-year famine, also is connected to Joseph.

The more straightforward reason that Joseph's name was not more prominent is the prophetic meaning of his name—"he will add, he shall increase." Instead of just one Hebrew or Israelite tribe being connected with his name, Joseph receives the double-portion honor among the twelve sons of Jacob in having two tribes directly connected to him through his sons, Manasseh and Ephraim. When Jacob announces prophetic blessings over his twelve sons and these two specific grandsons, he places special emphasis on Ephraim, the younger. Ephraim receives the blessing of exponential influence and effectiveness above that of his brother and uncles. This blessing is pronounced in literal form when Joshua, the son of Nun—of the tribe of Ephraim—is the one selected to lead all twelve tribes into the Promised Land following Moses's death.

This double-portion of tribal designations given to Joseph thus increased the total number of named tribes to thirteen. *(The same count of colonies in Warren's day.)* Because the tribe of Levi was designated as the group dedicated solely to YHWH and for the priesthood, it would not receive a large tract of territory when the land of Canaan was divided among the tribes. Also, during the wilderness wanderings between the exodus from Egypt and entering Canaan, Levi encamped around the tabernacle or Tent of Meeting in the midst of the other tribes. Thus, the number twelve was kept intact when describing the number and exact arrangement of tribal encampments in the wilderness and the number of tribes receiving land allotments at the end of their journey.

In the wilderness, the tribes of Judah, Issachar, and Zebulon camped under Judah's emblem of the Lion to the east of the tabernacle. To the north, the tribes of Dan, Naphtali, and Asher spread out under the Eagle emblem of Dan. To the south, Reuben, Simeon, and Gad were positioned under Reuben's ensign of the Man. And to the west of the tabernacle, the close-knit tribes of Ephraim, Manasseh, and Benjamin encamped under Ephraim's emblem of the Ox—representing the greatest beast of burden and servitude, encapsulating strength, status, and thus costly sacrifice.

The Lion, Ox, Man, and Eagle are emblems of tribes and creatures having supreme symbolic significance in prophecy and spiritual dimensions spanning the ages. And in this divinely directed camp layout, Ephraim and Manasseh were to be situated as the westernmost tribes—the sons of Joseph looking east at dawn across the entire encampment of the Hebrew people, at the rising sun and the resultant silhouette of the tabernacle. And in the evening, the children of Ephraim would look west and watch the curtain of light close over a distant coast beyond the horizon and the Great Sea (Mediterranean) it contained. The final rays of light would trail past the Rock of Gibraltar, shimmer across the vast Atlantic Ocean, and close out the account of that day on a Western Hemisphere containing other tribal encampments and great civilizations centered around sacred mounds and pyramids.

———•———

When the Israelites broke camp to travel to their next desert destination, Moses, Aaron, and the Levites—shouldering the Ark of the Covenant— would lead the way, followed by *Judah's group* of the Lion, *the first full tribe to move out* on the advance to new territory. Another set of Levites, carrying the tent canopies of the tabernacle, would go next, followed by Reuben's group under the Man emblem. The final group of Levites, bearing the tabernacle altars and other furnishings, would proceed in the middle of the massive caravan. *Ephraim's group*, with the Ox ensign, would *head up the second half of the tribes* following this third and final contingent of Levites and tabernacle items; the Ox thus following in the footsteps of the altar, incense, and utensils of sacrifice. The final group, that of Dan, Asher and Naphtali, under *the Eagle*, would make up *the rear flank of protection* comprised of more than 100,000 fighting men *ready to defend against any surprise attack.*

———•———

Upon reaching the Promised Land, Ephraim and Manasseh received unique land allotments. Manasseh is the only tribe that is apportioned land on both sides of the Jordan River—the blessing as the firstborn of Joseph. On the eastern side, it inherited the Land of Bashan—the northeasternmost territory of all the tribes—including what is known today as the Golan Heights. Its geographical relation to the others is similar to what New England (Massachusetts, which then included Maine and New Hampshire) represented to the other colonies. It was the region of the dawn land, the place where the Israelites would first catch a glimpse of the rising sun across the Levant. And like the Mohawk people, they were the watchmen and keepers of the eastern door—adjacent to the rest of the Fertile Crescent to the north and east, especially modern-day Syria.

On the western side of the Jordan and in the heart of Israel, Manasseh received a large portion of land that included Shechem and the mountains of Ebal (to the north) and Gerizim (to the south). Shechem was where Abraham entered this land of promise and first built an altar—the spot where the Abrahamic Covenant was sealed (Genesis 12:1–7). It's the place from which Joshua read aloud the commandments as Moses had instructed, with curses (from Mount Ebal) and blessings (from Mount Gerizim) issued to emphasize Israelite obedience to these precepts (Joshua 8:30–35 and Deuteronomy 27). The last chapter of Joshua relays his final instructions to the tribes after gathering them again at Shechem following the conquest, and it closes with the bones of Joseph finally being laid to rest at this strategic site (Joshua 24:32).

Ephraim's territory was just to the south of Shechem and the land of Manasseh. The tribe was situated in the middle of Israel and contained the city of Shiloh, where the tabernacle was placed with the Ark of the Covenant (Joshua 18:1). Thus, the land of Ephraim contained the religious center of Israel from the time of the conquest through the period of the Judges, up until David captured Jerusalem and relocated the Ark. With its central location and its eastern city as a prime gathering spot for decisions and guidance, Ephraim, like colonial Pennsylvania, could be considered the keystone state of the tribes. Shiloh, meaning "tranquility,"[3] was the ancient Israelite equivalent of the city of brotherly love (Philadelphia).

Boston, Massachusetts Colony | Spring 1774 to Spring 1775
Intolerable Acts and Undeniable Resolve.

Following the Destruction of the Tea in December 1773, British General Thomas Gage waited out the winter and moved in May 1774 from army headquarters in New York to Boston. The unthinkable actions of the Massachusetts colonists in defying British mandate and destroying property could not go unpunished. Boston would be used as an example for anyone else thinking they could disregard the king's authority and Parliament's dictates.

Between March and June 1774, as additional troops moved into position at Castle William and throughout Boston, Parliament enacted several measures collectively known as the Coercive Acts,[4] which the colonists dubbed the Intolerable Acts. The acts included closing Boston's port until the cost of the lost tea had been collected, stripping Massachusetts of its 1691 provincial charter, shifting the location of trials of British officials from Massachusetts to other jurisdictions under the guise of fairer hearings, and more expansive and intrusive quartering of troops throughout the colonies. Meant to punish and coerce the Massachusetts colonists into complete subjection to British rule while sending a broader message, the legislation had the opposite effect on a people desiring a rational and representative form of government.

The implications of this sweeping legislation reverberated across the other colonies to such an extent that Virginia's George Washington and George Mason wrote the Fairfax County Resolves[5] in July 1774 to protest Great Britain's overreach and called for a gathering of colonial delegates (a congress) and an association of the colonies to organize against any further Parliamentary aggression and importation of goods.

Joseph Warren and George Washington were men of similar understanding and intuition: the Boston Committee of Correspondence under Warren's and Samuel Adams's leadership had suggested just a month earlier that it was time to form an intercolonial congress.[6] Similar to Washington's Fairfax Resolves, Warren introduced the first draft of the Suffolk Resolves (named for Boston's Suffolk County) in a September multicounty convention in Massachusetts. The Suffolk Resolves described the current state of British intransigencies and how the colonies in joint fashion should address the situation and develop a defensive military posture. Warren's reliable friend and ally Paul Revere couriered the resolves to the First Continental Congress in Philadelphia. On September 17, 1774,[7] Congress endorsed Warren's resolves, which bolstered colonial unity, shifted the paradigm toward self-reliance and national independence, and set the stage for an earth-shattering revolution. With Philadelphia being the cradle of democracy (really a republic), Warren planted the seed that led to the birth.

Like his ancient forebear in Egypt, Joseph Warren found himself in the middle of empire-adjusting events having countless ramifications for generations to come. He had a gift for seeing situations not just as they were but as they would unfold. For example, the final article of the Suffolk Resolves laid the groundwork for the patriot alarm and the mustering of militia to confront any enemy maneuvers.[8] That the Continental Congress would adopt these Resolves, especially this article about employing armed resistance to British military missions, was a watershed event. From the Boston Massacre in 1770 up through the Destruction of the Tea in 1773, many decision makers in the other colonies thought the Massachusetts band to be a bunch of hotheads and a boisterous rabble itching for a fight. Now, through the face-to-face deliberations in Philadelphia and the Suffolk Resolves sitting before them, the true and dire situation was clear. As Benjamin Franklin had presciently adjured his fellow countrymen since the 1750s, it was time to "Join [unite], or Die."

Within seven months of Congress's adoption of the resolves, Warren and Revere were the ones faced with activating the patriot alarm that led to "the shot heard 'round the world."[9] And through Warren's decades' worth of training, trials and testing, he was thrust into the center of the day's politics and preparations for a conflict that spanned seven-plus years. Had Joseph Warren, in partnership with Samuel Adams, John Hancock, John Adams, and others, used the previous years to prepare the people and provisions for what lay ahead as Joseph of Egypt had wisely done? If so, liberty awaited their posterity through the threshold of bloody battles against a world empire. If not, then they would all hang from trees as the penalty for treason.

—————•————

As a close friend and confidante of Samuel Adams, Warren was one of the original members of the Long Room Club and Sons of Liberty who helped form the first Committee of Correspondence as described in chapter one. Eventually springing up throughout the Massachusetts countryside and other colonies, these committees coordinated responses to royal officials, established collective actions such as planning the First Continental Congress and forming militia units, and organized provincial conventions for the election of colonial leaders. As the revolution evolved, provincial congresses—like a joint organization of today's state legislature and governor's office—replaced these correspondence committees.

Joseph Warren became the first president *pro tempore* of Massachusetts's Provincial Congress—one of the highest positions in the colonies at the time. With John Hancock, the official president, being absent most of this crucial period to serve as a delegate and then president of the Continental Congress in Philadelphia—why his name is front and center on the Declaration of Independence— Warren often found himself carrying on the duties of president of the colonial province that was the bull's-eye of British aggression. He was the linchpin to all facets of the Massachusetts revolution remaining focused and synchronized in preparation for the looming confrontation. Through all this activity and coordination, Joseph Warren became the leader of Massachusetts, the principal colony dealing with the political and military crisis standing at the colonies' doorstep.

Besides the original Committee of Correspondence, other committees formed for specific purposes, especially in and around besieged Boston. Not because of his own posturing or position seeking, but due to his technical competence and servant-leadership style, Joseph was a key figure in the Committee of Donations and the Committee of Supplies and became chairman of the Provincial Committee of Safety.[10] He served on the Committee of Donations to receive, organize, and distribute food, money, and other necessities to those in Boston most affected by the port closure and the military siege. His role as primary coordinator of commodity management and distribution, along with sending letters of appreciation to the benefactors, is reminiscent of the Egyptian Joseph, who gathered and then dispensed the grain during the prophesied years of hardship.

His leading role on the Committee of Supplies involved obtaining and securing military matériel (weapons and munitions) and other provisions in the event provocations reached the level of armed resistance and retaliation. Warren was integral to the storing of supplies at Concord (one of the reasons the British set out for this site in April 1775) and other strategic locations outside Boston. He also worked closely with Benedict Arnold, whom the Provincial Congress promoted from Captain to Colonel,[11] in formalizing and executing a plan to bring cannons and other artillery from Fort Ticonderoga—a stratagem that George Washington and Henry Knox were later credited with carrying out.

The Committee of Safety acted as the executive arm of the Massachusetts Provincial Congress. Chairman Warren's role on this committee plus that of Supplies put him at the center of making critical decisions related to movement of major weaponry (i.e., cannons), formulating the stipulations of activating and ordering a militia, and eventually developing the strategy for battle fortifications on the hills north of Charlestown in June 1775. To Joseph's dismay, the troops built the redoubt on the smaller and more vulnerable Breed's Hill than the more imposing and defensible Bunker Hill.

It was this Committee of Safety that, along with its larger provincial congress, met in Concord in early April 1775[12] to finalize militia regulations and prepare for the inevitable. They adjourned on April 15, and Samuel Adams and John Hancock remained in the Concord and Lexington area to rest and recalculate a few days before their trip to Philadelphia for the gathering of the Second Continental Congress. It also wasn't in their best interests to be in or near Boston because General Gage had posted warrants for their arrest—one of the reasons the soldiers marched in their direction on that eventful night of April 18, 1775. Warren also lived under the threat of arrest,[13] but his duties as a physician to a beleaguered city kept him from being absent for too long. He would endure the dungeon if need be in order to fulfill his Hippocratic Oath. And it was his background and interactions as a physician that made his role unique among the other Founders.

Throughout all of the demands on his time and energy, Dr. Warren's medical practice remained open until the shots of April 1775 sounded. The reach and realm of his interactions and ability to heal were unlike any other. As renowned scholar-physician Dr. Samuel A. Forman so aptly states:

There has never been an American physician's practice quite like Joseph Warren's, either before or since the Revolutionary era ... he cared for future American presidents, governors, and senators; enemy leaders; and children, women, and men from the highest station to the most humble slaves to people associated with the occupying British army. His students went on to found Harvard Medical School and the Massachusetts Medical Society and to govern the state of Massachusetts.[14]

Through his decades of caring for small and great alike—including the opposing forces of the Tories' governing elite with their British military troops and the Whig Sons of Liberty firebrands with their farmer/craftsman militiamen—he knew how to walk with kings while maintaining the common touch.[15] He had the ear of the eighteenth century's Herods and Pilates while attending to the pressing needs of the Boston North End's ill and impoverished.

As noted in chapter one, it was through the smallpox inoculations that Joseph became the dear friend and family physician of John and Abigail Adams. One of the most moving accounts is associated with their seven-year-old John Quincy Adams, who later became the sixth president of the United States. The young lad had severely damaged a finger, most likely requiring amputation if it had been attended to by any other physician. In his latter years, the former president recalled fondly how Dr. Warren's expertise coupled with tender care preserved the finger instead of hastily removing it in order to attend to more pressing matters in Cambridge at that time.[16,17] It recalls a first-century situation in the Garden of Gethsemane the night before death, that a servant's detached ear was miraculously healed by the One being led away to a mock trial, torture, and execution (Luke 22:49–51).

His apprentices included Samuel Adams, Jr., the only son of Sam Adams, and William Eustis, who later served in President James Madison's administration as Secretary of War (during the War of 1812) and became governor of Massachusetts.[18] Dr. Warren instilled not only medical knowledge and skill in his students but also a sense of duty, honor, and service before self. All of these young men answered the call and beheld the blood of battle as physicians in the American War for Independence.[19] They continued the work and expanded the reach of their teacher, who soon gave his "last full measure of devotion."[20]

Through his medical expertise, mastery of communication, and top Masonic position (as we shall see later), Dr. Warren commanded the respect and affection of people from all walks of life, political persuasions, and stations of responsibility on both sides of the conflict for American autonomy. He could converse and hold court with crown-appointed governors and generals while on the same day attending to the basic humanitarian needs of the Boston populace. He faced betrayal and hardship, loneliness and long nights, yet endured to the point of rising to exponential prominence in the Provincial Congress and its executive committees. Joseph Warren used the years of plenty to prepare for the years of peril. He did so to spare his brothers in arms and their families from the looming devastation that was intended to devour them. He set the tempo for a people desiring a new life in a new era by transforming their quick sprint of desire into a methodical marathon of determination.

Now there arose a new king over Egypt, who did not know Joseph. (Exodus 1:8)

While it meant a time of trouble for Joseph's people (the Israelites), it was more detrimental in the long run to the secular society that forgot the man who had saved it from destruction and the One who gave Joseph the ability to interpret dreams and provide sound instruction.

Born in 1747, a Scottish advocate and historian named Alexander Fraser Tytler, also known as Lord Woodhouselee,[21] was of the same generational epoch as Joseph Warren. There is presently much online debate about a concept on democracy and an eight-stage cycle dealing with a nation's rise and its ruin that many have attributed to him. Some blogs and online articles credit Alexis de Tocqueville with the insights due to his 1835–1840 work known as *De la démocratie en Amérique* (*Democracy in America*).[22] There also is heightened interest in the analysis of Sir John Glubb; a twentieth-century British soldier, scholar, and statesman; who described a similar pattern of decline within a 250-year period when looking at the average age of empires over the past four thousand years.[23]

Whether it was Tytler, Tocqueville, Glubb, or an amalgam that generated the overall determination of the 200- to 250-year sequence is of little relevance here; further source sleuthing and digital due diligence hinge upon the reader's discretion. The primary point is that there is an alarming amount of evidence that powerful and prominent societies tend to transition from devotion and dedication to a desire for decadence and a disdain of absolute truth.

What is of primary concern is that leading figures of the day voiced their trepidation about human self-government bereft of morality. George Washington, John Adams, Thomas Jefferson, Benjamin Franklin, and other Founders admonished future generations to maintain their moral footing more than anything else. When a people and those they place in power forget the Joseph principles of self-sacrifice and servant-leadership based on biblical precepts, then Egyptian archetype taskmasters will arise.

Moral relativism produces a ship without a rudder, tossed to and fro by the whimsical winds of cultural confusion and waves of self-indulgence. One need only reflect upon the ancient empires[24] that imploded under their own largesse, fiscal irresponsibility, and anything-goes culture. Intolerable acts will again seep into the governing paradigm, and united resolve based on courage and conviction will be found wanting. It's the vacuum that invites modern-day Caesars and cesspools. Only the direct and divine intervention of a Deliverer will do.

The roles of a father are many
from the rising to setting of sun.

And a land under siege adds new hurdles
to tasks that never seem to get done.

With steady hands and a matching gait
he imparts wisdom and the patience to wait.

For the time will soon come
when life's drumbeat of battles will hum,
to test the character defining one's fate.

The following chapter is dedicated to my father,
Ronald E. Strouse, who passed from this mortal realm
on August 30, 2019—the same week I began
formulating the subsequent prose that
hopefully would make him proud.

After military service, he earned his master's degree in
English education from Temple University in Philadelphia,
causing me to smile yet cringe in hoping that
all of the grammar contained herein is correct.

PHOTO COURTESY OF MY TWO SONS: KALEB AND KEATON STROUSE

CHAPTER FIVE

EGYPT AND A DELIVERER

Nazareth, Galilean region of Roman-controlled
Palestine | ~ 4 to 1 BC | Matthew 1–2

A lowly carpenter transports a toddler King through Egypt.

JOSEPH, A SIMPLE CARPENTER CRAFTSMAN IN NAZARETH, FOUND himself in a situation similar to Abraham in that he was about to receive a miraculous son of promise. The vast difference is that Joseph wasn't longing for this new addition to the family just yet, nor did he see the surprise development at first as a blessing to celebrate or a joyous occasion to proclaim throughout the village. He and Mary, while betrothed, weren't yet fully married—and this Child in the womb wasn't his.

Joseph would serve as the protector and
provider, but not the progenitor,
of a little One in swaddling cloths.

His entire outlook on the matter drastically changed when an angelic emissary relayed the midnight message that changed his life (Matthew 1:20–23). Despite being of the tribe of Judah, Joseph's ancestral family settled in the northern tribal territories upon their return from the exile in Babylon and Persia instead of going south into the Jerusalem, Bethlehem, or Hebron region. Thus, when Caesar Augustus called for the taxation census, Joseph had to make an arduous journey south to Bethlehem, the city of his renowned ancestor David.

Even the lineage lines in Matthew and Luke tell their own interesting story. The book of Matthew, written mainly for a Jewish audience, describes the fulfillment of prophecies connected to the long-awaited Messiah. It begins with a lineage description from Abraham to Joseph through King Solomon's royal line. Joseph's father is named Jacob, repeating the ancient Abraham-Jacob-Joseph pattern. The first two chapters focus on Joseph and four dreams, a mixture of promises and precautions. This too reflects upon the Joseph of Genesis's outlook and instructions through dreams from a heavenly origin. It's an unveiling of a New Testament Joseph assigned a great cause and related cautions, of dreams and distant Magi.

While the angel addresses Joseph as "son of David" (Matthew 1:20) to acknowledge his royal heritage, the curse proclaimed by the prophet Jeremiah (22:24–30; 36:30) against Solomon's seed inheriting David's throne nullified Joseph or his physical offspring from this prominent position. Joseph still could have walked around with an air of entitlement as a prince in an occupied land, but he focused on being a carpenter and care-giver for a young maid, carrying in her womb the most Royal of royalties. And while Matthew focused on Joseph, we turn to Luke to learn more about this young woman named Mary.

If Matthew's description could be termed a consideration of dreams, Magi, and stars, then Luke's could be seen as that of a decree, a maidservant, and shepherds. While Matthew starts his summary with a lineage, Luke waits until the end of a lengthy introduction (the final part of Luke 3) and goes in reverse order. Beginning with the young couple in Nazareth, Luke looks back and doesn't stop at Abraham. He describes the family tree all the way to the original trunk and root system of the first man, Adam.

Luke's genealogy doesn't just differ from Matthew's in order and scope; it describes a different line of succession under King David.

It doesn't go through Solomon, but through Nathan, another son of David and Bathsheba. Many theological scholars point out that the Luke version is Mary's royal line, a princess in whose body there was no curse of continuation to the throne—a willing vessel of honor in which to incubate the King.

While Matthew was trying to show a strong Jewish and Davidic connection and qualification, Luke was intent on an all-encompassing fulfillment of prophecy for every tribe and tongue related to the One who would finally vanquish Eve's slithering nemesis that introduced distrust, disunity, and sin. Thus, Luke 3 brings to light and fulfillment the words of the Creator to Eve in dispensing a promise in the midst of curses in Genesis 3—through the woman: "her Seed ... shall bruise your [the serpent's] head" (Genesis 3:15). This Seed was planted in Mary and would grow into the Conqueror of sin and the Deliverer from death for both Jew and Gentile.

One final note of interest in the two lineages is that the name Joseph is mentioned three times by Luke when describing the patriarchs of the blessed and promised lineage, but not once in Matthew's gospel account except for the concluding name—the man with simple yet steady carpenter's hands. Luke also shows a similar repetition of various renditions of the name Matthias (Matthat, Mattathiah, Mattathah), and we shall see later how these two specific names (Joseph and Matthias) figure prominently in Acts 1 just before a spiritual explosion in a Feast of Weeks (Shavuot) fulfillment.

After Jesus's birth and visitation by the shepherds who were responsible for watching over and heralding the arrival of spotless lambs for sacrifice, Joseph and Mary prepared for their presentation at the temple to comply with the Mosaic law of Leviticus 12. They circumcised Jesus on His eighth day of breathing earthly air and awaited the completion of Mary's forty days of purification. Luke's account of what they offered as the burnt offering displays their financial status and provides a clue as to whether the wise men had yet arrived and bestowed upon them the expensive gifts of gold, frankincense, and myrrh.

Leviticus 12:6 states that a new mother, to complete her purification, is to bring to the priest a lamb for a burnt offering and pigeon or turtledove as a sin offering. Verse 8 adds that if she can't afford to bring a lamb, the mother can substitute a second pigeon or turtledove for the burnt offering. Luke 2:22–24 focuses on the sacrifice of two birds, noting the current state of this young couple's meager means when bringing the infant Lord of Glory to His ornate sanctuary.

———•———

The two birds as in Noah's day – a day of beginnings
for those with very little in earthly possessions.

———•———

After the temple presentation and sacrifices, Joseph and Mary return to Bethlehem to await the next set of instructions on what to do with their new addition to the family and enormous responsibility. It is during this period of waiting that the Magi from the East make their way through Jerusalem and Herod to a humble abode in Bethlehem. Matthew describes the scene (2:11) of the wise men coming to a house—a normal residence, instead of a stable—where they find Mary and a little Toddler, by whom and for whom the stars, planets and their satellites move in precise clockwork fashion to glorify and proclaim (Matthew 2:9; Genesis 1:14; Psalm 19:1–4).

The whereabouts of Joseph during this encounter of worship and gift giving is unclear, as he isn't mentioned until the dream sequence in subsequent verses warning the wise men to exit stage right back to their Eastern origin and for Joseph, Mary, and Jesus to exit stage left into Egypt. The gifts from the Magi provide the means for the next phase of their journey. Under cover of darkness that night, Joseph bundles up Mary and Jesus to set out on their trek to a country he's heard many intriguing and eerie stories about but has never seen.

———•———

And just as in Egypt during Moses's infancy, when a despotic leader sought to eradicate any threat from the burgeoning yet subservient male population (Exodus 1:15–22), Herod ordered the execution of all boys ages two and under in Bethlehem and surrounding areas. Death and destruction hunted for the precious life when evil men tried to protect their status and positions at all costs. In the Moses situation, a Joseph had been instrumental in the preservation of multitudes from many nations and the arrangement of a major prophecy fulfillment (Genesis 12:13–14) hundreds of years before the deliverer and lawgiver arrived. In the Jesus situation, a Joseph was central to the preservation of humanity spanning millennia and the fulfillment of many Messianic prophecies as he transported the ultimate Deliverer and Lawgiver across the sands of the Sinai. Joseph, Mary, and Jesus came to the land where Moses had floated in a small ark of bulrushes for protection among the reeds and where the blood of the first Passover lambs was shed and spread across thresholds to spare countless lives from destruction. The final and conclusive Passover Lamb took in the landscape with His own yearling eyes.

Out of Egypt I called My Son.
Matthew 2:15 | Hosea 11:1

Following the death of Herod, Joseph again received instruction in a dream to move his family.[1] The last time a prominent Joseph and new generation were leaving Egypt for the Judean hills, the emancipated Hebrews carried Joseph's bones to his final resting place in the promised land after bearing his sarcophagus on their shoulders during the forty years of wilderness wanderings. This time, Joseph was personally transporting the Christ child on foot without undue delays or detours. This departure and journey from Egypt had a prophetic correlation with what Hosea first penned about the children of Israel, but drew its complete fulfillment in this second, smaller albeit more significant exodus. It was a transition from the Old Testament and its (Mosaic) covenant to the New Testament and a covenant in which the Word and all related conditions and complete propitiation became flesh[2] to dwell among us and execute the transaction in the purest of blood.

The divine intent of Israel's exodus out of Egypt was for the Hebrew people to become an exceptional nation, a model of covenant relationship and salvation to the other countries and cultures of the world—showing forth the truth, grace, and delivering hand of God against all odds and the distractions of false deities and idols that entice. But the Israelite tribes often made mistakes and many times failed miserably.

Jesus was the embodiment of what Israel was supposed to be.[3] Just as He was the second Adam[4] sent to redeem and restore where the first Adam had fallen short, Jesus fulfilled the various phases of Israel's preparation for her purpose by being preserved from death by Herod (Matthew 2) as Moses had from Pharaoh to become the deliverer; being baptized in the Jordan (Matthew 3) as the Israelites were baptized in the Red Sea;[5] and going into the wilderness for forty days, like the forty years of wilderness wandering, to endure trial and temptation (Matthew 4). Jesus came to complete and fulfill all that Israel was destined to perform. That's why Matthew uses Hosea's prophecy about the exodus. And there was a Joseph in a strategic, supporting role in both scenarios, intrinsically involved in the realm of serving as the catalyst for original placement, preparation, and provision.

The dream to leave Egypt and return to Israel didn't specify where exactly the family should go. It is easy to assume that Joseph would return to his hometown of Nazareth[6] in the Galilee region, as that was where his family and support structure were, along with established business connections in the carpentry trade. But his focus wasn't on convenience, comfort, or career. He knew he had been given the greatest of assignments in raising a special Son, somehow destined to become the Messiah and the King of the Jews. Jerusalem in Judea, not Nazareth in Galilee, was the center of religious instruction and advanced learning. Therefore, Joseph initially aimed for a Judean location,[7] as his son's training took preeminence over everything else. Joseph's flexible attitude and considerate perspective in not hard-headedly planning to return to Nazareth sheds light on his unassuming nature and not being prone to presumptuous sins.

Joseph's final dream[8] directs the placement of where he should establish a home for Mary, Jesus, and other future children during the formative years of their upbringing. It was not to be in Judea, but in what the contemporary religious leaders considered a secular backwater contaminated by the site lying on one of the Empire's major East-West trade routes that linked Damascus to Ptolemais and then on to Rome.[9] In fact, the phrase "Can anything good come out of Nazareth?" (John 1:46) was a widespread perception of this location. Moreover, the entire Galilean region was considered incapable of producing any spiritual leadership (John 7:52).

In this northern residence, the brunt of Jesus's early instruction in the scriptures, beginning with the Pentateuch, then the prophets, and finally the hagiographa,[10] would rest upon Joseph due to the custom, especially with sons, that the father had primary responsibility for training the children. For the Savior and Son of God, a carpenter, not a scribe or a Sanhedrin member, was selected to serve as the mentor for this one-of-a-kind Prodigy. It would negate any acclaim going to the rulers of the day in Jerusalem that this Jesus became prominent because of their tutelage (John 7:15). And a carpenter's shop introduced the skills of woodworking and the sting of slivers decades before His shredded torso burned against an unforgiving beam and His hands were pinned against a limb fashioned by fellow craftsman of His trade.

———•———

After Luke's account of Jesus at age twelve in the temple, the Gospels go silent about His adopted father. What exactly happened to Joseph continues to be a matter of curiosity and speculation. The main and most important point about Joseph's absence as Jesus began His earthly ministry is that the story wasn't about him. He fulfilled the supporting role of protector and provider for the family until the sons (Jesus, James,

Joses, Simon, and Judas)[11] came of age. He was selected to be a servant in the shadows of the light and action on the main stage. The absence of Joseph allows full focus on a heavenly Father's interactions with Jesus in His next and final human phase on earth.

And this heavenly engagement comes into full view and focus when the Spirit, represented by a dove-like Presence,[12] descends once again upon a watery realm signifying death, burial, and the cleansing of Creation. It was there in the Jordan River with John the Baptist at Jesus's baptism that the dove made its final approach onto a landing zone of One robed in human flesh for mercy's and grace's sake. As Noah and Japheth had done in preparing and overseeing the operation of the ark for protection and passage, Joseph had performed similar responsibilities in Jesus' early years so that this encounter, like the determined dove of Genesis, could finally take place to usher in a new and glorious dispensation.

Boston and Philadelphia | Fall 1774 to Spring 1775
Arousing courage in others requires a cadence,
and service requires a servant's heart.

Boston, the Puritan epicenter of religious piety and instruction for the American colonies, boasted one of the highest literacy rates of the Western Hemisphere. Sunday sermons were not just heard, but newspapers such as the *Boston Gazette* and *Boston Evening–Post* would print them for the populace to read and reread the following week. It was here that a young Benjamin Franklin began his career in the newspaper business and polished his hand at writing under the pen name *Silence Dogood* in order to get published in his brother James's *New–England Courant*. Boston and nearby Cambridge, containing Harvard—originally established as a religious school—were like the New World's Judean sector of that day. Pastors, teachers, lawyers, and other professionals gained their training from this hub of higher learning.

But Boston, as a primary port city, also had strong secular and mercantile characteristics, as did Nazareth, because it was located along a major trade and transit route. It was affectionately referred to as a blue-collar "Beantown" by sailors and tradesmen due to the baked bean and molasses concoction that would warm the stomachs and souls of many weary New Englanders contending with bitter winds and stormy seas. It was a place for silversmiths, carpenters, longshoremen, fishermen, and British lobsterbacks—the menacing Roman soldier-like antagonists of the time. It was a quintessential tale of two cities with the best and worst of times colliding in dramatic fashion.[13]

King George III and Parliament acted like Caesar Augustus and the Roman Senate with their penchant for control, order, and taxation across the provinces of their empire to fuel their fleets and footmen. And General Gage, who replaced Governor Hutchinson as the new governor general a few months after the 1773 Destruction of the Tea, operated as the King Herod instiller and enforcer of martial law. The Intolerable Acts, Tory spies, and British troops were the instruments of revenge he used as a Vise-Grip on the people and pursuits of the province. His aim and instructions were to subdue and conquer—to ensure all subjects of the sovereign were kept in check so that no one rose up to challenge the king's authority. And there was a Joseph right in the middle of safeguarding the infant idea of independence from the brutal intentions of oppressive overseers more interested in power and rule than their countrymen's dignity.

Gage was so intent on total control that it drove him not only to execute the siege of Boston but also to pursue any perceived threats to the kingdom. The arrest warrants for Samuel Adams and John Hancock as Sons of Liberty ringleaders and the desire to disarm the villages led him to mobilize and move the troops toward Lexington and Concord on that infamous April night. And Joseph's Sons of Liberty alarm network was akin to the dream warnings sent to wise men to take another route and to a carpenter to make strategic moves.

Speaking of the best and worst of times, it also was a period of changing times, literally. Like the conversion from BC or BCE to AD or CE as a result of Jesus's physical presence on earth and signifying the tectonic shift in epochs, the world's main calendar (Julian) changed to the current Gregorian system in the Middle Ages for most of Europe. The Julian calendar, named for Julius Caesar, was instituted by the Roman emperor in 45 BC[14] to align time with the solar year (earth's orbit around the sun) instead of the lunar cycles (moon's orbit around the earth). The Gregorian calendar, named for Pope Gregory XIII, instituted an improvement in the calculations of leap year adjustments and became the norm in 1582[15] for most European countries following Roman Catholic dictates. The British empire, predominantly Protestant, wasn't under the auspices of the pope and thus remained on the Julian calendar until 1752, when England acquiesced and concluded that having two global calendars to mark world affairs was untenable, and special dates on the British calendar were becoming more misaligned with the seasons due to the errant leap year formula.

Why all of this is mentioned here is that when this major calendar shift occurred for England and her colonies, it was the same period (1751–1754) when Benjamin Franklin and other leaders began to implore the importance of colonial unity (see chapter one). It marked the creation of Franklin's "Join, or Die" imagery and the beginning of a paradigm shift that builds up the confidence of people and tears down the imposing façades of empires. It also caused the birthdates of America's Founders to shift by one year and eleven days. For example, George Washington's birthday was February 11, 1731, on the Julian calendar, but later changed to February 22, 1732,[16] on the current Gregorian calendar. It upended recordkeeping and brought about a transformation in thinking about making a mark during one's days on earth instead of just marking off the days as a form of accomplishment.

And just like the birthdate quandary of the 1700s, the proper year to assign to Jesus's birth ironically remains one of the greatest enigmas of human history. One thing that hasn't changed is the Hebrew calendar, which is based on a solar-lunar relationship—the interaction of a true light source coupled with an object reflecting that originating light. One eradicates the darkness during the day, and the other pierces and overpowers the darkness of the night.

With respect to carpentry (the trade Joseph taught Jesus) and the more advanced engineering and building guilds, two interesting aspects come into view. The first is associated with the name of the location where the First Continental Congress met, what was discussed, and when it occurred. The second is connected to a secret order that placed Joseph Warren at the center of major decision making and directive giving during the formative years of the country's founding.

Many tourists in Philadelphia flock to Independence Hall, originally known as the Pennsylvania State House, because it is the birthplace of the Declaration of Independence and the U.S. Constitution—the site where the Founders drafted, debated, and signed these two documents that English-language adjectives fall short in adequately describing. Very few places on earth carry such weight with respect to their impact on human history.

> But a similarly significant yet less frequented
> and photographed structure
> sits just two blocks to the east on Chestnut Street.
> And it served an important yet often-overlooked role
> befitting its Joseph-like character and charm.

The aptly named Carpenters' Hall, headquarters of the Carpenters' Company,[17] was where the delegates for the First Continental Congress met in the fall of 1774. They did so due to the perception that the Pennsylvania State House might have too many Tory sympathizers and spies observing and undermining the proceedings. Within Carpenters' Hall gathered representatives from twelve of the thirteen colonies, including George Washington, Patrick Henry, Richard Henry Lee, Samuel Adams, John Adams, John Jay, John Rutledge, and Christopher Gadsden. The only colony not participating was Georgia, stemming from strong Loyalist leanings among her leaders and overall populace. Exactly twenty years before, Franklin's "Join, or Die" serpentine image of the colonies presciently showed all but one aligned for coming together. The one missing was the southernmost colony of peanuts, peaches, and pecans.

In relation to Independence Hall, Carpenters' Hall is smaller and more obscure than where the later and greater debates took place and where the major documents were signed that the National Archives Museum now prominently displays. But its overpowering presence and importance is that it was the birthplace of birthplaces. It produced the original debate and declarations of unity when Paul Revere delivered the Suffolk Resolves on Warren's behalf. And it was the site where the great orator Patrick Henry put tangible effect to the feelings of many when he declared, "I am not a Virginian, but an American."[18] It cradled the paradigm shift of men from different locations, skills, and backgrounds coming together to confront a challenge no single colony could overcome alone. A microcosm of this mind-set in recent history was when all of the players on the US men's ice hockey team realized they were playing for their country, not their colleges, and went on to win the gold medal in the 1980 Winter Olympics after beating the highly-favored and four-time defending champion Soviet Union. Carpenters' Hall in Philadelphia was the site of a 1770s-era Lake Placid moment that struck a nerve and solidified determination to take on the world's reigning empire and its imposing red army.

The Suffolk Resolves, embraced by the First Continental Congress, were the linchpin in rallying and connecting all of the delegates in a common cause. Drafted and championed by Joseph Warren for adoption at the local, provincial, and continental levels, they led to a revolution, not just of government structure and function, but of how people began to see themselves and their place and importance as part of the congregants in this world.

In reflecting upon the timing when the first congress convened, the recently adopted Gregorian calendar really doesn't mean much. The congress gathered at Carpenters' Hall on September 5, 1774.

But looking at the one calendar that hasn't changed over the past three thousand-plus years—the aforementioned Hebrew calendar—an intriguing aspect unfolds. September 5 of that year was Erev Rosh Hashanah or the eve of Rosh Hashanah/Yom Teruah. The ending of one civil year and the beginning of the next, marked by the blowing of trumpets and major gatherings. It's the beginning of the Days of Awe in the month of Tishri. The day of a shout, the day of a blast, the day of a proclamation—hello, Patrick Henry and Joseph Warren. It is the only major Jewish holiday (holy day) that is connected with a new moon (*the beginning* of a Hebrew month) as the other Jewish high holy days occur later in Tishri and in the middle of the spring months. This new moon phase, in simultaneously marking the start of another month and entire year, represented the reset of a major time component and the initial days of a new era.

And following much discussion and debate, the Congress adopted the Suffolk Resolves on September 17, immediately following the highest Jewish holy day, Yom Kippur (the Day of Atonement), the most solemn and somber day of introspection and reflection. In the wake of Yom Kippur, people proceed with renewed devotion and dedication to a higher calling and more significant purpose.

On the heels of Rosh Hashanah, Yom Kippur, and the adoption of the Suffolk Resolves that year came Sukkot, the week-long Feast of Tabernacles. Its name is connected to the *sukkot* (booths or tents) that Jewish adherents celebrate in during this time as a reminder of the quick deliverance from Egypt and Providence's daily provision during their trek through the wilderness to the Promised Land. Moreover, the temporary structures remind humans of their fragile and temporary existence in tabernacles of flesh—leading to a deeper understanding that life's purpose has to mean more than just possessions and prominence.

Whether the Founders realized it or not, their timing in initially establishing consensus and forging a way ahead in the First Continental Congress aligned with a schedule and realm larger than their own and that of mere Gregorian clockwork.

Many historians attribute the delegates' collegial agreement and adoption of the Suffolk Resolves as one of the primary precursors for the Declaration of Independence.

———•———

With respect to advanced carpentry, architecture, engineering, and the camaraderie of these crafts, there comes into view an organization dedicated to the furtherance of these arts and sciences, the brotherhood of such pursuits, and a larger mission scope to be attained. Many scholars and historical records recognize that key figures such as George Washington, Benjamin Franklin, Paul Revere, John Hancock, George Mason, James Otis, Thomas Paine, and James Madison were Masons. Masonry being an international order, many British officers in besieged Boston in the 1770s were associated with this entity as well. And rising in prominence in the middle of these opposing yet connected factions was the doctor, instigator, organizer, committee chair, and provincial president *pro tem*, Joseph Warren.

———•———

This brief focus on Masonry is neither an
endorsement nor denouncement
of it or its influence in the founding of the United States.
It is merely intended to show the sway that
Warren had due to his position
over other Founders and many British officers simultaneously
during the formative years of a nation that
became like none other before it.
One would be wise not to delve into conspiracy spelunking,
fearmongering, or getting sidetracked with other aspects of an
order that will not be a topic of concern in eternity's realm.

———•———

In the early 1700s, the fraternal order of brotherhood and service to community known as Masonry gained a foothold on the new continent. Ironically, Boston was where the first lodge (St. John's) was established in 1733.[19] With its roots in the British Isles, the American version became known as Freemasonry with its ideals of liberty, the dissolution of strict class strata, and emphasis on free enterprise. With many prominent men and Founders being Freemasons, this order influenced much of the country's early history. And due to its renowned allegiance among members and its strict hierarchy, Joseph Warren's unique position in his final years of life is most intriguing.

In colonial America, many men became Masons to establish and strengthen an esprit de corps with others in their community, form professional networks, and foster a structured means of addressing the needs of the impoverished. That third point was a prominent characteristic as government support structures and safety nets didn't exist back then, and many children's hospitals and other philanthropic works still around today are living testaments of those early efforts. All of this appealed to a young and aspiring Dr. Warren in 1761 when he joined the St. Andrew's Lodge of Masons in Boston.[20]

If Joseph Warren was merely interested in career progression and community position, he would have joined the more prestigious and elite St. John's Lodge, the aforementioned first in the colonies, that boasted among its members Governor Hutchinson's family and Warren's own mentor, Dr. Lloyd.[21] But its prestige was connected to Loyalist and Tory political power and policies—which were anathema to Joseph. Instead, he gathered with the likes of Paul Revere, John Hancock, and Benjamin Edes* at St. Andrew's, the organization that owned the Green Dragon Tavern and met there in its Long Room on the second floor[22]—the same space where the Long Room Club of Revolutionary War fame gathered, with many of the same constituents.

---

* Benjamin Edes, publisher of the *Boston Gazette*, was one of the original Loyal Nine members,[23] the group that presaged the Sons of Liberty and Long Room Club—the catalysts for independence and unity throughout New England and then all the colonies. Benjamin, a fitting name to be closely connected to a Joseph (the only two sons of

Rachel in Genesis), was a leader in his own right and close confidant and supporter of Joseph Warren. In the years ahead, there came another Benjamin—one who had different loyalties and ended as a traitor to the cause.

———•———

Shortly after joining the Masons, Dr. Warren had to attend to other pressing matters such as the smallpox epidemic in 1764, which focused his time and energies elsewhere. But even in situations such as the smallpox inoculations and treatments, he was forming unique bonds with influential people across all political persuasions and leadership positions. Recall that through his medical care, he became close friends and the family physician of John Adams' family and that of Governor Hutchinson plus others in the upper echelons of society. But the suffering he witnessed of people from all walks of life gave him an even greater understanding and keen sense of human frailty and the significance of each living, breathing, and departing human soul. It was his drive to make a difference in communal responsibility and medical advancement that drew him to the Masonic ethos.

When the smallpox scourge was in its waning days the following year, Dr. Warren returned to Masonic functions with renewed vigor. His natural leadership style and energetic ingenuity, coupled with an unwavering sense of duty and doing what was right, propelled him to strategic rank. And his prime placement was magnified by St. Andrew's unique position.

While St. John's was the first Masonic lodge in North America, it operated under the modern versus ancient order. Wanting to stay true to the original Masonic code and conduct, St. Andrew's, as the first in the Western Hemisphere under the Scottish Rite Ancient pattern, received its charter directly from Masonic headquarters in Scotland.[24] Under this unique arrangement of direct authority from the Scottish headquarters, Joseph Warren was appointed the provincial Grand Master,[25] noted as the first with this title,[26,27] for those Masons following the ancient rite discipline throughout New England, and later, all of North America. The latter footprint and influence were due to Joseph gaining a more expansive and semiautonomous charter designating St. Andrew's in Boston with Grand Lodge status for the continent.[28] Through all this expanding prestige, Joseph and his Masonic brothers interacted with people of various posts and perspectives, from staunch patriots to Tory loyalists and British soldiers who had their own traveling lodge units. Thus, the authority of St. Andrew's Lodge in Boston over the new continent and Joseph's title would have granted him heavy sway and influence with many patriot leaders and Founders. Joseph's rank also commanded respect from the British military officers who issued, and the disciplined foot soldiers who followed, all orders—whether emanating from the mouth of a monarch or grand master.

But Joseph Warren wasn't interested in power for power's sake. The system he facilitated at St. Andrew's was one of collaboration, even in trying to form common bonds with St. John's elite and exclusive club. Joseph's clout and connections as Masonic leader and revered medical doctor throughout the land afforded him the opportunity to work across ideological trenches and broker common ground between conflicting factions until the last resort of rifle shots became a necessity. Joseph's writings, speeches, and closed-door conversations were aimed at forging understanding and a rational way ahead for all inhabitants on New England soil.

While Revolutionary War historians often connect Joseph Warren's rise in prominence with his close friend and mentor Samuel Adams, Adams was not a Mason and shied away from relationship-building enterprises with those wearing red soldiers' uniforms. Joseph had the aptitude and foresight to seek consensus and serve as a mediator with Governor-General Gage, which was vital during the initial phase of the siege of Boston when brokering the passage of people and provisions in and out of the city. In April 1775, while Adams and Hancock remained in Lexington due to warrants for their arrest, Joseph returned to the beleaguered Boston to work in the full light of lanterns and candles and also in shadows of concealment for those souls who were about to clash with an empire's most formidable forces.

Whatever the remaining annals of late eighteenth-century history and Masonry relay about Dr. Joseph Warren, let it be known that the humble, pragmatic, yet powerfully positioned grand master was admired by many as a peacemaker and collaborator rather than an antagonist and disrupter. If he had seen fit to attend the gatherings in Philadelphia for the First or Second Continental Congress, his renowned reputation and oratory skills would have carried the day. Had he chosen to remain far from the Bunker Hill battlefield and lived to see the year 1776, the delegates who debated the Declaration of Independence would have paused with respect each time Dr. Warren rose in that sacred hall to give testimony to reason and resolve. Had he continued as a general officer through the heavy years of the war and sat with George Washington in 1787 at the Constitutional Convention, no gavel would be required to silence the onlookers whenever he moved to speak. But it would be his blood, not his breath, that provided the vibration across wooden floors and against plaster walls to spur men of destiny to act with conviction and consensus. His life produced the drumbeat that created a cadence—a cadence that configured the courage needed to confront the most confounding of challenges.

But in similar fashion to the Joseph who guided Mary and Jesus in those frail and formative years, Joseph Warren would not be present at the crescendo and climax of the story. His frame would fade after the stage had been set for the main actors to transition into central positions. His purpose completed once the cadence was well under way, Joseph's silhouette shifted behind the curtain of mortality so as not to overshadow the succeeding act. And his absence from further human acclaim is what catalyzed the subsequent steps of Adams and Jefferson and Washington.

Whereas Dr. Joseph Warren and silversmith Paul Revere dispatched many significant messages via the thundering hooves of an elegant and enduring steed, Joseph the carpenter and Mary the maidservant relied upon the steady gait of a small yet sturdy donkey to deliver the ultimate Message.

Each player has a name,
and each contributes to the game.

A team is a band of brothers.
You fight as one against all the others.

For strategic games that are set in war,
reliance is crucial like never before.

But with a traitor in your midst,
all thoughts and movements tend to get blitzed.

He creates battles without and within.
The most painful blows delivered by kin.

So set your heart upon the prize,
and let no distraction confront your eyes.

CHAPTER SIX

SILVER AND A SALUTATION

Bethany, Jerusalem, Gethsemane and Upper Rooms |
Winter to spring transition, AD 30[1]

Matthew 26:14–16 | Mark 14:10–11 |
Luke 22:1–6 | John 12:4–6; 13:2, 26–30

Focusing on silver is shortsighted, and treachery turns on the traitor.

T HERE SEEMS TO BE A VILLAIN IN EVERY STORY, ESPECIALLY THE
traitorous kind within the close circle of cohorts and confidants.
With the name Benedict Arnold showing up as an esteemed and close
acquaintance, one could safely wager that it was only a matter of time
before his diabolical ruse was set in motion. But irony also plays a part
in high-stakes outcomes, and so it did in the form of namesakes in the
1770s … and some 1,740 years before.

It's hard to imagine that someone hand-picked by Jesus the Christ—
who spent three years witnessing His miracles, teachings, and daily
encouragements—would be able to betray Him. Judas Iscariot saw
Jesus calm the sea, heal the sick, walk on water, and wake Lazarus
from the dead. He watched this Rabbi do things that no human had
ever done or even imagined were in the realm of the possible. He had
the vantage point to know that it wasn't just an act during the day or

a sleight of hand to stir up a following for fame or fortune. It was a genuine ministry that would cause the other apostles to go willingly to their deaths as a result of not denouncing, but more emphatically pronouncing, what they had seen and heard.

And yet, Judas somehow missed it. His stupefying decision provides a clue as to how Adam and Eve could make the original wrong choice of giving in to temptation and deception while they enjoyed walking in the garden and having a direct relationship with their Creator on a daily basis. Beware of the tempter, for somehow Eve, Adam, and Judas were curiously drawn to the sensual—lured by the temporal rather than the eternal. Humans tend to fixate on the mammon rather than the heavenly Manna—the One who not only multiplied the loaves and fishes but *is* the life-giving and -sustaining Bread.

What's even more perplexing is the name and place associated with Jesus's betrayer. Judas is the New Testament version of Judah—"adore/ praise Jehovah." It was a common name in that day—Jesus even had a brother with the same—especially if the male was from the tribe of Judah. The original namesake was Leah's fourth son; Jesus's half-brother Judas was Mary's fourth or fifth son as well (Matthew 13:55; Mark 6:3).

The surname Iscariot, which most scholars translate as "from K'riot or Kerioth,"[2] relates to a town approximately twenty miles south of Jerusalem near present-day Hebron. It was close to the tomb of the patriarchs and matriarchs; where Jacob rests with Leah; the land of Judah's inheritance (Joshua 15:20, 25); and just over the hills from where David tended flocks, learned how to slay bears and lions, and developed his first psalms.

If any of the twelve inner-circle disciples were of the same tribe as Jesus, the odds are that it would have been Judas Iscariot. The other eleven were from the Galilee region in the northern part of Israel.[3] If any of them—hardened fishermen, tradesmen, or tax collector—were familiar with the praise and worship of YHWH (Yahweh), it most likely would have been Judas.

Growing up in the land of Judah and with a name proclaiming the praise of Jehovah, Judas's actions create an enigma about betrayal.

But his proximity to saving grace and the utter disdain of it ironically also enlighten our understanding. If one could see, hear, and touch the life-initiating Logos that walked among us and that person still turned away, then it's no wonder that people left to their own devices today find it easier to seek silver than the Savior.

The turning of the tables hinged on the love of mammon and misplaced loyalty. Judas wasn't interested in a movement to set people free; he was intent on a revolution to punish Roman oppressors. When the renewed kingdom of Israel wasn't materializing in the way or at the speed that Judas had presumed, he decided to take the initiative to set things in motion. And in doing so, he turned against the King, not understanding this divine Royalty would first come as a Lamb to purge people before returning as a Lion to pursue and protect them.

Jesus sought out and selected Judas Iscariot. The Messiah wasn't fooled or mistaken on the selection. He loved Judas just as He did the other disciples. Everyone has ample opportunity and access—even when their utter rejection of mercy and grace looms on the horizon. It's the greatest of liberties—to be handed the opportunity to choose freely between good and evil.

Not only was Judas one of the twelve inner-circle apostles, but he was next to Jesus in the Upper Room for the Last Supper. Judas's hand received the morsel of bread from the hand that, in less than twenty-four hours, would be pierced by an iron spike because of his decision. Even in the mere moments before his final act of betrayal, Judas was sitting next to salvation, not more than an arm's length away.

Judas wasn't relegated to a fringe seating arrangement in a far corner of the room. He was front and center on the world stage next to the One who could hold the Orion Constellation in the palm of His hand and part the Red Sea with the blast of His nostrils. Yet a mere thirty pieces of silver seemed more impressive during the days leading up to the point when Judas allowed the light in his soul to be replaced by utter darkness.

———•———

Many of Jesus's disciples were called apostles because of the messenger meaning. The terms *apostle* and *angel* denote the same type of emissary—"one sent on an errand."[4] In Acts 15, there was another Judas, surnamed Barsabas (a name to remember), who, with Silas, went with the apostles Paul and Barnabas to Antioch. This Judas Barsabas was dispatched by the council of the church at Jerusalem[5] to deliver decrees to the believers at a destination where the term "Christians" was first used. His work behind the scenes helped Paul and others promulgate a message that turned the world upside down (Acts 17:6).

Inappropriate intentions produce erroneous errands

Sadly, Judas Iscariot was a different type of apostle. He began formulating how to take matters into his own hands when Jesus began speaking more emphatically about death and sacrifice instead of the decor and splendor of an earthly kingdom. Judas was motivated by position while Jesus kept the focus on purpose. As the keeper of the purse, or treasurer in today's lexicon, Judas was sometimes absent from the group to handle money matters. The other disciples became accustomed to him being gone—and Judas grew comfortable with being away. Consumed by life's cares and business that morphed into routine busy-ness, Judas began running the wrong errands for the wrong reasons.

Jesus was a threat to the established order and the religious elite. He called out the hypocrisy of the Pharisees and Sadducees and their fixation on the Mosaic Law rather than on pleasing the Lawgiver and Liberator. These religious leaders of the day—the chief priests, scribes, and elders (Matthew 26:3)—began conspiring about how to get rid of Him. They knew outright removal would cause an uproar among the people because of His popularity and innocence, especially when throngs were in Jerusalem for the Passover observance. They needed an insider accomplice to work behind the scenes to remove this threat swiftly, by stealth. And Satan knew which apostle had a proclivity for secrecy and subversion (Luke 22:3–4). And so a deal was struck— money for the Master. Deliver Him and crush the rebellion before it takes hold and preserve the status quo.

At night, under cover of darkness, Judas greeted Jesus in Gethsemane and kissed him, but it was purely lip service—his heart and soul were miles away, having been foolishly traded for financial gain. The object of his praise and devotion became diverted and distorted, until he arrived at the place where he no longer was walking with the Lion of the Tribe of Judah but was consumed by an impostor lion who goes about "seeking whom he may devour" (1 Peter 5:8). There is a Lion to befriend and follow as British author C. S. Lewis so eloquently portrayed in *The Chronicles of Narnia*, but there are others to corner and kill as exemplified by one of David's mighty men in 2 Samuel 23:20.

It all comes down to knowing how to approach the type of lion one is dealing with. In the 1770s, there was a roaring lion across the Atlantic Ocean that was set on destroying any vestiges of liberty—to thwart a rebellion and keep everyone in submission. Were there any brave souls, blessed by Providence, who could successfully confront and conquer the British beast? Historic annals describe these men and women and their ultimate victory, but first, Joseph Warren would have to contend with a traitor.

IMAGE COURTESY OF PUBLICDOMAINVECTORS.ORG
(CROWNED LION 47743).

Upper Rooms and Councils of Committee,
Massachusetts Colony | 1768–1778
*Benjamin should have been like a brother, and
Church should be a unified body of believers.*

Of the twelve sons of the patriarch Jacob, Joseph and Benjamin were
the closest, being the only two of his beloved wife Rachel. In the heat of
battle and the trials of life, a brother is there to help bear the burden and
overcome adversity (Proverbs 17:17). It was previously stated that the
Sons of Liberty were the original band of brothers. To one another they
pledged their lives and sacred honor. They would either go through
the fire together to reach the sweet shore of liberty or would swing in
solidarity from adjoining gallows; at least that was the understanding.

It was an understanding of brotherhood birthed more than 150
years before, about forty miles south of Boston, along the Massachusetts
shore. At a place that became known as Plymouth Colony, pilgrim
passengers from the *Mayflower* disembarked in 1620 to begin a new

life by relying on Providence and one another. One of those passengers was Richard Warren.[6] His daughter Elizabeth (Warren) would marry a Mr. Richard Church, and they would have a son named Benjamin.[7]

This Benjamin Church was commissioned by Plymouth Colony Governor Josiah Winslow to develop a military force to work with and learn from Native American allies to confront the threat of hostile tribes.[8] Sadly, the primary tribe on the opposing side in King Philip's War (1675–1678) was the Wampanoag—the people who had befriended the original pilgrims under the direction of their great leader Massasoit and kept them from starvation in the settlement's early years.

Throughout this war and under the tutelage of Native American strategists, Colonel Church trained his forces, the predecessor of the US Army Rangers,[9] to use cover and concealment as battlefield tactics instead of the European practice of open and direct battlefield formations. This new method of warfare would serve the Colony of Massachusetts well exactly a hundred years later when Minutemen and militia would have to answer the call of duty in driving the British back to Boston on April 19, 1775.

Colonel Benjamin Church was the great-grandfather[10] of Dr. Benjamin Church, a distinguished and trusted physician in prewar Boston. Dr. Church thus hailed from a land south of Boston with a lineage steeped in sacrifice, Puritan praise for the Almighty, and an innate sense of duty and honor. All of this was reinforced during his studies at Harvard, where he was the roommate of another future Son of Liberty, John Hancock.[11]

An esteemed Harvard graduate and respected surgeon, Benjamin Church became a member of the cloistered Long Room Club in the upper rooms of a print shop and tavern. His close associates and trusted friends welcomed him into several Sons of Liberty initiatives. As Samuel Adams was in the process of rallying colony-wide support and solidarity in 1768 to oppose the Townshend Acts and influx of British troops, Benjamin was part of a small committee including Joseph Warren and John Adams that reached out to Whig sympathizers in England for support.[12] He also supported Joseph (the committee chair) and John in preparing instructions for local representatives at Faneuil

Hall and resolutions for Governor Bernard's consideration regarding the untenable burden of excessive taxation and additional troops.[13] Benjamin became a brother-like figure to Joseph—a fellow physician driven by the ethos of the Hippocratic Oath. They were two men in a whirlwind of looming revolution, a time when the local populace looked to them for resolute integrity and reliable instruction.

On March 5, 1770, the Boston Massacre shocked and incensed the city. Dr. Benjamin Church was one of the first at the scene to render medical aid.[14] He and Joseph went home that cold and dreary night with their clothes soaked by the blood of the slain and injured. The next day, Benjamin found himself on a new committee with Samuel Adams; it formed out of necessity to meet with acting Governor Hutchinson to discuss what had led to British troops firing upon fellow citizens and the need to separate the soldiers from the civilians.[15] Benjamin's presumed devotion to the cause and speaking skills were such that the Sons of Liberty selected him to give the oration at the Old South Meeting House in 1773 to commemorate the third anniversary of the massacre.[16] The crowd esteemed him as a polished and principled orator who could precisely verbalize the high points of a cause that was quickly coalescing around them.

In the relatively uneventful interval between the March 1770 melee and the December 1773 dumping of the tea, Benjamin became an integral part of the patriot inner circle consisting of Samuel Adams, John Hancock, Joseph Warren, and Paul Revere. This core group continued to carry forward the conviction of maintaining their rights as British citizens against the excessive force and intimidation of crown-appointed officials and the brutish soldiers under their control. Benjamin joined Samuel Adams and Joseph Warren in preparing correspondence to Governor Hutchinson and to serve as one of the main emissaries to His Excellency on behalf of the population throughout the province.[17]

As 1772 drew to a close, Benjamin Church was selected as one of the five founding members of the Boston Committee of Correspondence facilitated by Samuel Adams.[18] Through this committee, the Whigs and patriots of Boston shared ideas and updates to other towns across the colony and to other colonies across the continent. Upon its formation, the committee prepared a three-part report about the colonists' rights, how the British government had violated those rights, and how other towns could create similar committees to share insights and updates throughout the region.[19,20] Samuel handled the first section, Joseph the second, and Benjamin the third. Benjamin's task was to compose guidance that encouraged other towns to form these committees of correspondence, and he was chosen for the duty because of his eloquent ability to effectuate participation and teamwork.

Joseph authored the portion of the report about the recent infringements on God-given rights, with special emphasis on personal freedom being an inalienable gift from the Almighty.[21] This bold and comprehensive report reverberated across the land and became an exemplar for other documents yet to come, such as Thomas Paine's *Common Sense* and Thomas Jefferson's Declaration of Independence. John Adams, as part of the Declaration's composition committee, later recalled how similar Joseph's list of British infringements was to Jefferson's emphasis of natural rights and list of grievances.[22] The Declaration was written in 1776 while Joseph's work was from 1772, so it's easy to see who emulated whom.

———·——

During this time of formulating thoughts about true freedom, other ideas and intentions were beginning to take shape. Loyalists were so named because of their loyalty to the Crown and the British way of life. They and the Tory traditionalists—intent on maintaining the rigid social strata in line with English culture—were opposed to any paradigm shift that proposed all men were created equal. Seeing a major confrontation was in the making, Benjamin Church began hedging his bets. An apparent opportunist saddled with debt, he wanted to ensure he was on whichever side won while also profiting in the process.

Seemingly stalwart and steadfast, Benjamin Church appeared to be an avid patriot and friend, but appearances can be deceiving. And he wasn't a true Loyalist as his character was anything but loyal. Dr. Church's financial burdens fueled a motivation for material gain instead of a solid footing to stay the course in a life-changing movement that was gaining momentum. Benjamin's behavior of living beyond his means with an expensive estate south of Boston became a millstone around his neck like the rope Judas Iscariot finally felt around his.

———•———

At the Old South Meeting House in March 1773, Benjamin was front and center with other leading patriots for the third anniversary of the Boston Massacre as the designated orator for the solemn occasion. Sadly, he used his standing among the people and Sons of Liberty for a duplicitous purpose behind the scenes. While he walked with patriot leaders in the light of day and gathered with them around the candlelight at night, he had fomented friendships with government officials in the shadows of 1771 and 1772.[23] Within two years' time, Benjamin was secretly partnering with those forces that had unleashed the musket balls of lead that created the wounded and the dead on that infamous winter night of 1770.

> Like Judas, somewhere in a three-year period of time, Benjamin's heart turned to the other side—to the environs of the establishment and the scene of the status quo. He didn't courageously switch affiliations as if by some major shift in personal conviction. He deceitfully remained attached to both camps, thinking to influence and manipulate all the actors across the stage for his maximum benefit.

In the fall of 1774, the committee coordination in Boston exponentially increased and took on an even greater meaning now that the First Continental Congress was established and operating in Philadelphia. Benjamin was with Joseph at the momentous Suffolk Convention as a delegate that September where the famous resolves were crafted and then couriered by Revere to the Congress at Carpenters' Hall. The following month, Joseph's and Benjamin's combined work on the Massachusetts Provincial Congress and its Committee of Safety[24] became even more significant as John Hancock, the other Bostonian in this new governmental structure, was also heavily involved in the leadership of the Continental Congress. Thus, Joseph and Benjamin became the de facto patriot leaders of the province in a time of upheaval.

The Committee of Safety established the guidelines for organized defense of the communities throughout Massachusetts, developed an alarm system to quickly warn surrounding areas of any threatening troop movements, and determined how to acquire and where to hide weapons if the day came that required armed resistance. Dr. Benjamin Church was privy to all these sensitive discussions, and so the British would know where to go (Concord) on April 19, 1775, to confiscate the Patriot arsenal. It was like having Judas carry the money bag.

In the months leading up to that fateful April dawn, Joseph Warren and his Committee of Safety ordered and obtained military supplies to be dispersed to various locations (Cambridge, Concord, Salem, etc.) outside the Boston stronghold.[25] This committee was one of the primary avenues for the Sons of Liberty to prepare the people, mainly the militia and rapid-response Minutemen, for what was coming.

March 1775 marked the fifth anniversary of the Boston Massacre, and Joseph was the featured speaker. With him at the dais that day in the Old South Meeting House were Samuel Adams, John Hancock, and Benjamin Church.[26] In addition to the large crowd gathered for the occasion were numerous British military officers to observe the proceedings. Arrest warrants had been issued for Adams, Hancock, and Warren—interestingly not for Church—but it was unlikely that Governor General Gage would execute the order given the likelihood of the outcry it would ignite among the people, especially on a day marking the heavy hand of those in military uniforms. The time of year and situation reflected similar schemes and overall reticence by Herod and the high priests when trying to remove a Thorn from their side. It was not the opportune time to make any sudden moves, as doing so would ignite a public insurrection on such a memorable occasion. They would rather conduct their business in the hours of darkness when the populace was tucked away at home, succumbing to human slumber.

One month later, in April 1775, that slumber was shattered by thundering hooves and Paul Revere's clarion call through the night that the British were coming. The fighting of April 19 and subsequent strategy sessions by the Committee of Safety precipitated the exposure of Benjamin as the dreaded informant. In all the various notes of correspondence and commands from the committee to the provincial forces in the wake of April's armed conflict, Joseph uncovered a damaging document attributed to Benjamin Church.

After the patriot militias had driven the British troops back to Boston, they had set up lines of defense in case the British executed another offensive on the surrounding towns. A mid-May note that Joseph received and read was a message from Benjamin to a patriot officer about moving his forces away from a strategic checkpoint near the Boston Neck land bridge to another location; it was an instruction that ran contrary to what General Artemas Ward had ordered.[27,28] Had Joseph not countered and corrected these deceptive instructions, the British would have been able to surprise and decimate the provincial forces by exploiting a gaping hole in their defenses. From the patriot perspective, there was no rational reason for Benjamin to be issuing this type of dangerous directive.

Erratic behavior and errant errands

It did, however, shed further light on Benjamin's erratic behavior, which arose just two days after the clashes at Lexington and Concord. On the evening of April 21, Benjamin insisted to Joseph and others on the Committee of Safety that he needed to go into the city for various reasons. A renowned biographer of Joseph Warren notes that this episode provided the "ominous overtones of a Judas among the Patriot faithful ... going off on a dubious errand into enemy-occupied Boston."[29] It was later learned that Benjamin had met with General Gage. For his informant services and acts of betrayal, the British paid him handsomely—more than he could have gained through normal channels.[30] The proverbial transaction of silver for sedition.

Later that year, another piece of correspondence was intercepted, and General George Washington had him arrested. Benjamin was tried and found guilty of communicating with the enemy,[31] after which he was stripped of his prominent positions, and his seat of authority in the provincial government was given to another (like that of Judas in Acts 1:20).

After several years of imprisonment, he was ultimately banished from Massachusetts. No longer a welcome member of society, Benjamin Church looked out over Boston Harbor for the last time in January 1778 as he boarded a ship for Martinique.[32] The vessel never reached its intended destination but was lost at sea. Suffering the demise of a Judas coupled with that of a wayward Jonah, Benjamin was swallowed not by an awaiting whale but only by angry waves.

Prepare the hill
for there ye will
see triumph, and legend, and lore.

Stand ye fast
for against the mast
comes a blast like never before.

The cannons rage
against troops of all age
from ships called men-of-war.

The Redcoats ascend
while farmers defend
and stand ready to settle the score.

The day will soon end
with all hearts to mend
for his brief life encompassed much more.

CHAPTER SEVEN

DEATH ON A HILL, LIFE IN THE TRENCHES

Golgotha, outskirts of Jerusalem |
Passover/Pesach, early spring, AD 30[1]

Matthew 27:57–60 | Mark 15:42–46 |
Luke 23:50–54 | John 19:38–42

Never was there such a life laid down so that others could carry a crown.

IN STARK CONTRAST TO THE EARLIER EVENTS OF THAT DAY, THE FINAL few hours of preparation before the Passover seder were silent and solemn. The shouts of the crowd for crucifixion, the crack of the whip in the scourging, and the eerie pinging of Roman hammers against iron nails to bring forth final screams of the condemned were now just distant sound waves. The three hours of darkness followed by the earthquake that rent the veil in the temple from top to bottom stopped idle conversations and exuberant exclamations from those who had plotted the death penalty and performed the execution.

Now all that lingered in the air on that barren hill were the final onlookers' moans of emotional agony mixed with the trailing scents of dust and death. With most of Jesus's disciples dispersed, just a handful of faithful followers stood wondering what would be done with His body still hanging there while the soldiers removed the other deceased convicts. If it had been any normal crucifixion day, the corpses likely would remain in place against the wooden beams for the birds to consume.[2] The other option, especially right before a high holy day like this (John 19:31), was to throw them into a common gravesite, the usual spot being in the Valley of Hinnom—Jerusalem's trash pit and refuse incinerator.

But all four Gospel accounts mention a specific individual, of the most unlikely sort, boldly approaching Pontius Pilate to ask for possession of Jesus's body. The main aspects relayed in Scripture are that he was a wealthy man from Arimathea, a member of the Sanhedrin but also a secret follower of Jesus, and one who had a new tomb in the most strategic place on earth. And of course, his name was Joseph.

Joseph of Arimathea, a man of means and distinction, had much to lose by publicly asking to take and properly bury the remains of the supposed blasphemer and insurrectionist. After all, the Sanhedrin had acted in supposed unanimous agreement[3] to condemn this Jesus to death for His outlandish claims and the perceived threat He posed to civil and religious order. But Joseph was not constrained by the authorities or raucous crowds as there were few, if any, other Sanhedrin members around to interfere during his conversation with Pilate that afternoon. Throughout the entire day's proceedings, the Jewish leaders abstained from entering the Gentile Praetorium so as not to defile themselves[4] before piously performing their duties related to Passover/ Pesach and the seven-day Feast of Unleavened Bread/Chag HaMatzot.

Nor was Joseph constrained by any vestige of conflicted contemplation. He had the opposite reaction to the turn of events than that of Jesus's inner circle of disciples, who scattered. While Simon Peter had openly followed Jesus during the three-plus years of teaching and miracles, this same bold and brash man denounced the Christ and fled when it mattered most—and the cock called his bluff. Swinging swords and boisterous rebuttals don't scare spirits determined to carry out dark missions.

Witnessing all that transpired that day, something happened inside Joseph that made him stand tall and remain stalwart in a realm where angels trod. When others headed for the exits, he stepped onto the stage and into the brightest of lights right on cue when the next crescendo of action was needed. He didn't stumble with confused thoughts, fumble with indecision, or mumble his lines—his conversation with the Roman provincial governor was crystal clear and concise. And the combined tally of audience observers would number in the millions when considering the four Gospel accounts and their reach across the globe over the past two millennia.

Whether Joseph of Arimathea abstained from the mock trial the previous night—the timing and procedures of which were inappropriate according to the Sanhedrin's self-imposed protocols—or if he served as a stupefied spectator, he was determined after Jesus' death to be on the right side of history. He wouldn't be caught flat-footed or dumbfounded anymore; he would be a man of purpose and action, even if it meant removal from a prestigious post in this temporary, mortal realm.

Only two of the Gospel writers (Matthew and Luke) provide details of Jesus's birth, but all four (Matthew, Mark, Luke and John) describe Joseph's involvement related to His burial. The fact that they separately saw fit to focus on those post-death hours, especially Mark who wrote things down shortly thereafter, provides some of the strongest and earliest proof of Christ's historical existence.[5] There are no competing claims of any viable substance among cultures or critics for what happened with the body. Also, all four writers put their credibility on the line by naming a precise person, a member of the Sanhedrin at that, because everything associated with this group was loathed by early believers. Many adherents and antagonists alike would be quick to call out any discrepancies with such specific statements; therefore, it wouldn't be the smartest way of devising a fictional account of what had occurred.

By going to Pilate for permission to take care of the corpse instead of just impetuously removing it from the cross, Joseph cemented in historical annals the fact that Jesus was indeed dead and not just in a state of extreme shock or comatose. If the Roman executioners, experts in crucifixion's dreadful results, were unsure of Jesus's medical status, then they would have broken His legs as they did with the other two criminals to accelerate the asphyxiation process. As visible proof of death, a soldier pierced Jesus's side to watch blood and water flow, not just ooze, out of the body cavity to prove asphyxiation had taken its deadly toll.

Pilate conferred directly with the centurion responsible for Golgotha's gallows as he wanted to be sure everything was completed and that haste wasn't getting in the way of death's door. Only after confirmation from the centurion did Pilate release the body to Joseph.

While Joseph's bold actions have inspired millions over the centuries, they also brought immediate encouragement to a fellow Sanhedrin member and another secret follower of Jesus. Nicodemus (John records) had previously met with Jesus at night to learn more about Him and His teachings, stepped forward to help Joseph move the body from Golgotha to the nearby garden tomb and prepare it for burial. He brought a mixture of myrrh and aloes in such a large quantity that the associated costs would be akin to a royal interment. At His birth, wise men brought myrrh to signify His priestly anointing and sacrificial mortality before He went down into Egypt. At His death, wise men brought myrrh to maintain His mortal frame as He went down and conducted final business in Sheol.

Jesus was placed in *Joseph's tomb*; it wasn't Jesus's tomb.
What He accomplished during that interval
in the realm of the condemned
means He also was deposited in *your tomb*, as a
death sentence's full and final payment.

The characteristics of Joseph's tomb fulfilled prophecy and established a sanitized buffer around this Mediator and Priest after the order of Melchizedek (Psalm 110; Hebrews 7:12–28). A priest was to keep away from an area containing the dead, and so Joseph's new and unused burial chamber provided the perfect sanctuary for Jesus's body to be placed in a pure state, undefiled by other decaying flesh or bones resting in ossuaries.

Jesus, the Good Shepherd and Sacrificial Lamb, most likely was born in Bethlehem's Migdal Eder (Micah 4:8; 5:2), the stone-structured Tower of the Flock, where shepherds brought expectant ewes in from adjacent fields to birth spotless lambs destined for temple sacrifice. The temple connection meant, according to rabbinical rules, that the stable-like enclosure had to be ceremonially clean for these specially designated sheep. Likewise, the stone-structured tomb for Jesus's combined work as High Priest and Slain Lamb had to be pure and undefiled. This humble carpenter's Son, the suffering Servant who had little in earthly possessions, was buried in a carefully prepared rich man's tomb as Isaiah (53:9) had prophesied more than six centuries earlier.

Whereas the "Silent Night" carol is sung to recall Jesus's birth, the more probable hushed evening of holiness would have been as dusk turned to darkness following His death. It must have been one of the most serene and solemn nights the earth has ever experienced.

When Joseph of Arimathea requested the body of Jesus, he unapologetically bore upon his shoulders a bold yet embarrassing responsibility of caring for the remains of the One who had claimed to be the Son of God with the power to overcome death but who now remained cold and lifeless. It was akin to Joseph the carpenter not shunning but remaining espoused to Mary after knowing she was pregnant in order to shield her from the heavy onslaught of public ridicule. Both Josephs stood in the gap to take on the brunt of humiliation while ensuring the needs of Jesus and Mary were met during the most vulnerable and poignant times of life.

The primary man present at Jesus's birth was named Joseph.
The primary man present at Jesus's death was named Joseph.

At Jesus's arrival, Joseph wrapped the newborn Baby in swaddling cloths and laid Him in a manger while Mary recovered from the exertion of childbirth.

At Jesus's departure, Joseph wrapped the beaten body in strips of linen and laid Him on a stone slab while Mary recovered from the agony of His death.

———•———

And the ultimate paradox: Through all the trouble of keeping Jesus's body pure and undefiled, Joseph became ritually unclean right before the high holy days of Passover and Unleavened Bread. He and Nicodemus could be considered the only people throughout history, besides Mary's previously mentioned forty-day purification period after childbirth, who touched Jesus and became contaminated rather than cleansed following the encounter.

The reason is that the Old Testament plainly states that coming in contact with a human corpse renders someone ritually unclean[6] (the highest grade of uncleanness) for seven days (see Numbers 19:11 and 31:19). In Moses's day, there were certain men in Numbers 9:6–12 who couldn't participate in the Passover activities and had to remain outside the camp for this very reason. They had to wait a full month before conducting something akin to a makeup session.

Thus, Joseph, the man who stepped forward to handle all aspects of Jesus's honorable burial, became tainted and separated from the Jewish nucleus of holy day gatherings in Jerusalem that weekend. But on the flipside, he and Nicodemus were the ones in closest contact and face-to-face observance of the prophecy-fulfilling Passover Lamb, of which all the others were just precursors and placeholders. Joseph transitioned from dwelling among the inner circle of prestigious men to operating within the sanctum of the Savior.

———•———

On the very day that this Savior was shedding His blood, soldiers were separating His clothes. They were more focused on the pieces of fabric spread across the ground than on the remnant of tattered flesh stretched out just a few feet above them.

Four soldiers and a seamless garment

Similar to relaying the account of Joseph of Arimathea, all four Gospels mention the soldiers dividing the clothing and casting lots (Matthew 27:35; Mark 15:24; Luke 23:34; John 19:23–24). Matthew and John connect the significance of this activity to fulfilling the Psalm 22:18 prophecy. John provides further detail about the soldiers evenly dividing things into four portions, thus giving the impression that four soldiers were involved in the transactions. The most intriguing aspect throughout history has been John's special mention of the seamless garment, called a "tunic" in the New King James Version (NKJV) and "coat" in the KJV, which also describes it as a "vesture" in Psalm 22.

Due to its uniqueness as one continuous fabric, the soldiers decided to keep the garment intact instead of cutting it and thus cast lots to determine who would be the fortuitous recipient. Its seamless, single-fabric depiction aligns with what Exodus 28 and 39 describe as one of the high priest's garments—the robe of the ephod.

> You shall make the robe of the ephod all of blue. There shall be an opening for his head in the middle of it; it shall have a woven binding all around its opening, like the opening in a coat of mail, so that it does not tear. (Exodus 28:31–32)

> He made the robe of the ephod of woven work, all of blue. And there was an opening in the middle of the robe, like the opening in a coat of mail, with a woven binding all around the opening, so that it would not tear. (Exodus 39:22–23)

It is one of the articles of clothing that the renowned first-century historian Flavius Josephus chronicles in his comprehensive work, *The Antiquities of the Jews.* Josephus notes that the high priest wore a long blue robe or vestment under the ephod; and he carefully and conspicuously makes the point that it was a singular and seamless article of woven fabric, not something consisting of two or more pieces.[7]

Throughout the tabernacle plan and intricate design of the temple, there were always three specific colors associated with the curtains, covering, and clothing—blue, purple, and red. If Jesus's seamless garment for which the soldiers cast lots that fateful day was something resembling the blue robe of the ephod, then a terribly beautiful color pattern appeared. The blue fabric, where it came in contact with that precious red blood, would have displayed the deepest and most meaningful purple hue human eyes have ever seen.

This renowned Flavius Josephus, at birth named Yosef ben Matityahu[8] in Hebrew or *Joseph* son of Matthias,[9] is unique among historians. He is regarded as the preeminent source of independent information outside of the Torah and the Bible on Jewish generations, life, and laws. His eyewitness reporting of what occurred in Roman-controlled Palestine shortly after Jesus's death up through the siege of Jerusalem and destruction of the temple in AD 70 is unmatched and has been used as the primary reference material in countless secular and religious tomes throughout the centuries to the present day. Josephus's writings are priceless as they provide the sole surviving record of firsthand accounts from this pivotal time in human history.

His exhaustive works *The Antiquities of the Jews* and *The War of the Jews* give us an extensive understanding of what the Pharisees and Sadducees thought and taught, how the cloistered Essenes lived, and what occurred in the tumultuous first-century revolt against Roman rulers. Written for Greek and Roman audiences, Josephus's *Jewish Antiquities* is a comprehensive Hebrew history from Creation to the Roman Empire's iron-fisted rule, while his *Jewish War* describes the attempt to wrestle free from that iron fist, including a determined people's final stand on a hilltop called Masada. Furthermore, and ironically as he was from a prominent priestly family in Jerusalem and himself a Pharisee, Josephus provides strong confirmation of the existence of John the Baptist, Jesus, and His brother James.

Born into one of Jerusalem's aristocratic families shortly after Christ's death, Josephus lived an interesting life before dying in Rome in AD 100.[10] Both his father and brother were named Matthias,[11] an intriguing arrangement when recalling chapter five's description of Jesus's genealogy in Luke 3 and the Joseph and Matthias selection process in Acts 1 (addressed in greater detail in chapter eight).

Similar to Paul, one of the most well-known apostles, Josephus received rigorous education and training to become a Pharisee, made Rome his final residence, and was a prolific writer. Both waged war and then went through a major conversion process. The difference between Paul and Josephus is that Paul initially wielded a sword against the early church, only to join it later and become one of its most ardent influencers. Josephus initially wielded a sword against the Roman Empire as a Jewish military commander in Galilee during the major uprising known as the First Jewish Revolt or First Jewish-Roman War (AD 66–70).[12] Following his capture and conversion to Roman citizenship, Josephus takes on the role of peacemaker and apologist on behalf of the Jewish people. It is this apparent switch to the Roman side and the eventual emperor Vespasian's favor upon him that caused many in Judea at the time to despise Josephus as a turncoat.

But with time, distance and deeper perspective, it's easier to envision Josephus acting as a pragmatic public servant standing in the gap between his countrymen and Vespasian the Roman. Where his loyalty lay was of the same pattern as that of Daniel's interactions with Nebuchadnezzar the Babylonian and Darius the Mede, like those of Ezra and Nehemiah with the Persian kings Cyrus and Artaxerxes, and reminiscent of the time and calling required for Esther with King Ahasuerus.

———•———

So not only did a prominent man of Jerusalem named Joseph
serve as the primary benefactor of Jesus's
body following His final breath,
but the most renowned historian of the age was of the same name

and described the land, creatures, and customs
of the atmosphere He breathed.

———•———

One Joseph cradled the remains of the Messiah.

Another Joseph captured the essence of the civilization
that was the cradle of the Mishnah.

———•———

Breed's Hill, outskirts of Charlestown | June 17, 1775
Stalwart in the trenches and standing in the gap so that others may live.

The redoubt was on the wrong hill.

Throughout the night, provincials from Charlestown, Cambridge, and the surrounding area built an expansive earthwork of defensive positions on the promontory overlooking Charlestown and the Charles River opposite Boston's North End. Across the water stood the steeple of the Old North Church—like a silent sentinel patiently waiting to observe what the dawning day would bring. Just a couple months ago, it was a beacon of two bright lanterns. Now, in the predawn hours of Saturday, June 17, 1775, it was just a dark silhouette of a structure sitting in the throes of a besieged Boston.

Time was of the essence. With the arrival of British generals Howe, Clinton, and Burgoyne, plus another 1,000 troops, Joseph knew General Gage would be emboldened to recalibrate the status quo and initiate offensives to expand the footprint of British martial law around Boston. In the days following the Lexington and Concord conflicts, Joseph had corresponded with General Gage on refugee movements and prisoner exchanges to ensure the safe passage of noncombatants into and out of Boston through the ominous checkpoints.[13] With Joseph's leadership responsibilities in the Provincial Congress and Committee of Safety, he had been in regular communication with Gage, the Crown-appointed overseer of the province, in the hope of averting any further

JOSEPH

hostilities and maintaining open lines of communication.[14] All such hope evaporated with that morning's mist.

Those who erected the redoubt meant well, but in their haste to prepare for the first major confrontation with the British Empire's combined might of its land and naval forces, the patriots essentially placed themselves within the paws and jaws of the lion. Their aim was to occupy and fortify the high ground throughout the Charlestown Peninsula, but Breed's Hill was a little too close to danger's doorstep. In strategic military terms, it would have been prudent to remain entrenched at Bunker Hill to protect the Charlestown Neck land bridge while also ensuring a safer distance from most of the British cannonade until the heavy artillery from Fort Ticonderoga arrived.

Breed's Hill, in contrast to the higher and more distant Bunker Hill to the northwest, was within easy reach of the British navy's arsenal and the army's arms and legs. It was only at sunrise, after a long night of building a fortification in the darkness, that it became clear just how near they were to the opposing force's full strength. The realization and magnitude of the moment hit them square in the stomach like the brutal thrust of a bayonet.

The major misplacement seemed to jeopardize in just a matter of hours all ...

The collaborative work Dr. Joseph Warren had done in the Committee of Safety; all

The intricate planning of the alarm system and intelligence-gathering network; all

The strategic discussions under the veil of secrecy of the Long Room Club; all

The brave sacrifices of the militia and Minutemen who confronted professional soldiers at Lexington and

- 89 -

halted their menacing advance at Concord, driving
the British back to Boston; all

The careful contemplation at the military headquarters
in Cambridge just a few hours before; and all the
courage and consensus of the volunteer soldiers who
came to stand in the gap and fight for their fellow
colonists and, to that point in the struggle, trusted
the wisdom and foresight of their leaders.

Establishing a fortress on Bunker Hill had been the object of
intense discussion and planning in the Committee of Safety and the
Massachusetts Provincial Congress.[15] The hill's height and distance
from the cannons on Copp's Hill and the imposing men-of-war on
the Charles River would allow the men to muster and defend from a
platform of strength instead of the vulnerable threshing floor of Breed's
Hill. But it was too late to adjust their footprint as dawn broke on
that mid-June Sabbath. With the sun's initial rays came the first signs
of a searing heat that would sap their remaining energy on this final
Saturday of spring.

Would the coiled serpent later emblazoned on Gadsden's flag and other
venerated standards stay and strike at the harassing boots of enemy
intruders, or would it slither away to perceived safety under the cold,
dark recesses of retreat?

Summertime temperatures came early that year, and the oppressive
heat of the past few days, combined with accumulated exhaustion
and the oscillating levels of adrenaline, took its toll on men in mortal
frames. After a few hours of precious and fleeting sleep, Dr. and soon-
to-be-commissioned Major General Joseph Warren struggled to his

feet following a late night of conversations and final deliberation with other members of the Provincial Congress at the political and military headquarters in Cambridge. He and Elbridge Gerry—who later joined the delegates of the Second Continental Congress in Philadelphia, signed the Declaration of Independence, helped draft the Constitution's Bill of Rights, and became vice president of the United States under James Madison—were the only ones at the house where the previous night's discussions had occurred.[16]

They bore the heavy weight of decision-making while their close confidants—Samuel Adams, John Hancock, John Adams, Thomas Cushing, and Robert Treat Paine—were at the Second Continental Congress pleading for unity and action to confront the British military's recent aggressions and martial law stalemate in Boston. Just three days before, on June 14, their explanations and arguments bore fruit as the Congress voted to create a Continental Army and selected George Washington as commander-in-chief the following day.[17]

While Joseph had yet to receive word about the Continental Congress's progress in approving the formation of an army and appointing a leader, he would have celebrated the news; he had been a major proponent of such action and the person they selected.[18] The Sons of Liberty knew they needed a Virginian in overall command to coalesce cross-colonial support for the war effort. And Washington, due to his credentials and character, was at the top of their list.

At the onset of the deliberations, Joseph dispatched Paul Revere to Philadelphia with a letter to Samuel Adams stressing the need for prompt action by the Congress in selecting a commander-in-chief. In his message, Joseph specified Colonel Washington for several reasons, including his exploits in the French and Indian War—especially during the Battle of Monongahela—coupled with his moral compass and humble demeanor.[19] General Artemas Ward, the commanding general of provincial forces at the time and serving alongside Joseph, was a good man, but his frequent ailments were viewed as an Achilles heel that they could ill afford to overlook.

In the interim, Joseph continued to serve as a placeholder in filling the executive leadership void for the New England province until the Continental Congress sent instructions of who would lead the army and how it would operate. However, he couldn't just bide his time in Cambridge waiting for word of who was chosen and for continental regiments to form and march north. British Generals Gage, Howe, Clinton, and Burgoyne already were on the move in and around Boston, and again, the patriots at the center of the conflict needed to confront the aggression or else be consumed by it.

Joseph was the one holding everything together in these tense and tempestuous moments by bridging the gap between military expediency and the proper civilian oversight of armed forces.[20] His stalwart focus on following the wishes of representative government, instead of devolving to dictatorial demands as the heat of battle loomed, paved the way for the future preservation of the union before there was any formal union worth preserving.

———•———

Joseph pushed through his pounding headache[21] to get dressed, gathered his things, and proceeded to the Charlestown Peninsula. He was informed, to his utter chagrin, that the foremost patriot fighting position was on the much smaller and extremely exposed Breed's Hill. Joseph made his way past messengers bringing updates back to General Artemas Ward at the Cambridge headquarters. He went first to Bunker Hill where General Israel Putnam, in charge of the battlefield, was overseeing the final preparations for the day's major engagement. Joseph, as the chair of the Committee of Safety, had spent many days and nights discussing such contingencies with Generals Ward and Putnam. And now the planning would transition to full execution in the hours before them.

Joseph and Israel prepare for battle

Joseph and Israel were well acquainted. The latter was a legendary veteran of the French and Indian War and recently organized and commanded the Connecticut militia. The previous summer, he brought

150 sheep from his farm as a donation to the impoverished in Boston suffering from the closure of the port as one of Parliament's Intolerable Acts.[21] While in town, he lodged at Joseph's house. The men had much in common, and Joseph was known for his hospitality and his prominent network of friends and key acquaintances.

Between the April 19 skirmishes in Lexington and Concord and the June 17 Bunker Hill battle, Joseph and Israel led several hundred provincial militiamen to repel British troops attempting to forage fresh supplies at Noodle's Island, northeast of Boston, on May 27–28.[23] This small but significant confrontation is known as the Battle of Chelsea Creek and was seen as a patriot victory in that the militia forces prevented the British from obtaining needed provisions while also causing the loss of HMS *Diana*.[24] The Continental Congress received word about the battle's success at the same time it was selecting the senior leaders of the newly formed army[25] and likely led to solidifying Israel Putnam's brigadier general rank in the transition from his militia leadership to the larger fighting force forming under General Washington.

All of it came to a surreal conclusion that June day on Bunker Hill as Israel acknowledged that Massachusetts's Provincial Congress had just proffered Joseph a major generalship. Israel turned to his friend and overall authority for guidance, given Joseph's new appointment plus his leadership roles in the Congress and the Committee of Safety, which had direct oversight of the province's military.

But Joseph hadn't come to serve in command status, as his commission was not yet official, nor was he interested in assuming any high-level position. Joseph's intent was to see the conflict firsthand and stand with the men where the fighting was most severe. If his recent decisions put people in harm's way, then he intended to walk among them and face the flying lead and shimmering bayonets shoulder-to-shoulder with the farmers, smiths, and servants. He knew decisions produced repercussions and was determined to personally see the matters of the day through to their conclusion, whatever the consequences might be. Whenever friends pleaded with him to be careful, Joseph was known to respond with, *"Dulce et decorum est pro patria mori"*—it is sweet and fitting to die for one's country.[26]

Israel said goodbye to his friend as he pointed Joseph to the Breed's Hill redoubt, under the command of Colonel William Prescott. It was the last time the two bid farewell.

Coming to volunteer while others vacate the cause

In much the same manner as Joseph's arrival and greeting at Bunker Hill, Colonel Prescott offered the position of command to Joseph when he entered the redoubt. And in much the same manner, Joseph declined. He was there to serve alongside those in the trenches. Joseph told both Putnam and Prescott that he didn't come to seek safety but to serve as a volunteer wherever he would be the most useful.[27,28]

Dr. Samuel A. Forman again provides a precise reflection about Joseph Warren, the day's meaning, and how it resonates for posterity's sake:

> Another aspect of the events unfolding on June 17, 1775, reveals Warren's personality and illuminates the American experience. Warren was twice proffered the field command of American forces, once by Putnam, and again by Prescott. He refused. Other men, with towering egos, would view themselves as the best leaders to direct the situation, political forms heeded only to the extent that they lent legitimacy to dictatorship. In contrast, by culture, Providence, and circumstance, the United States has not nurtured such dictators and demagogues. For the Warrens and Washingtons took as their models Roman Republicans Cato and Cincinnatus rather than Caesar.[29]

In a similar stead, the elder Seth Pomeroy was there to fill a frontline position despite also being appointed a generalship. The presence of these two high-ranking officials emboldened the patriots throughout the besieged redoubt under continuous bombardment by enemy artillery. That morning, the militiamen in that forward fighting position felt betrayed by finding themselves so close to the British forces. The presence of Warren next to them extinguished those feelings of resentment and ignited a renewed vigor to remain and fight.[30,31]

Throughout the day, Colonel Prescott had watched as approximately half the men deserted him. They left due to weariness from working all night to build the fortifications and—being new to warfare—were shaken by the constant barrage of British artillery from at least six different directions.[32] By mid-afternoon, Prescott was in desperate need of reinforcements and supplies as he repulsed the first two offensives by more than two thousand British regulars and marines with only about five hundred men and a dwindling amount of ammunition. But General Putnam was reluctant to send a significant amount of resources forward to this exposed area. He preferred the men withdraw and regroup to fight another day rather than expend any further militia forces in what promised to be a blood bath.

———

This American moment on Breed's Hill was the epic battle
that gave rise to the fighting spirit of the American Republic,
inspired paintings and pilgrimages,
and inserted in subsequent generations' subconscious
the backbone and stamina to stand strong
in other such situations such as
the Alamo in 1836 and Little Round Top in 1863.

———

The first major battle of the Revolutionary War, known in American history parlance as the Battle of Bunker Hill, is noted by many historians as the bloodiest of the entire conflict when considering the combined casualties. The patriots suffered the loss of 411 killed or wounded, while the British lost 1,054 men—the highest price of human life the British experienced during the war, especially within their commissioned officer corps.[33,34]

That fateful afternoon, the British mounted two unsuccessful attacks against the men on Breed's Hill and along the rail fence and other bulwarks running down the redoubt's left flank toward the Mystic River. These offensives were repulsed by patriot musket balls finding their targets, felling lines of marching redcoats as if they were on an ascending conveyor belt of mortal conclusion. In between the assaults, Joseph, in courageous medic fashion, moved across the redoubt under incoming artillery to tend to the injured.

In the previous weeks back in Cambridge, Dr. Joseph Warren and other leaders in the Provincial Congress had converted a deserted Tory mansion into a military hospital for any wounded during the April 19 conflict and subsequent skirmishes. The majority of the hospital's patients were redcoats, as Joseph was intent on providing the British regulars the same level of treatment as those fighting for liberty.[35] The decision to take up arms was to resolve a dispute, not with men consigned to fight for their country, but with the erroneous and egregious dictates of their leaders.

In fact, Joseph was well acquainted with many of the British officers and soldiers due to his prominent Masonic position along with his medical and political responsibilities. And several were his close friends, including Majors John Pitcairn and John Small. Major Pitcairn led the Royal Marines up the hill toward the redoubt and fell in duty to his country that day. Major Small made it over the redoubt in the final assault only to witness the demise of his friend and respected opponent, Joseph Warren.

Resolute in the face of retreat

The third assault on the redoubt in the day's waning hours was like the quiet yet crushing crescendo in the theatrical finale of a young man's last moments at just thirty-four years of age. Joseph's length of time on earth was almost identical to that of the famous miracle-working Galilean. In both situations, the orders of an empire's provincial rulers

(General Gage and Pontius Pilate) were executed and completed. *But it didn't mean the end of the story.*

Smoke continued rising from the remains of Charlestown, which General Howe set ablaze to neutralize the snipers who had plagued his left flank. Compared to the thunderous explosions throughout the day, the hillside went quiet as patriot ammunition was expended and the surrounding cannons and field artillery held their salvos when the redcoats overran the earthworks. The silenced iron barrels joined the Old North Church steeple, both of their missions complete, in quietly observing the conclusion of the matter.

The only sounds on Breed's Hill now were officers issuing rapid commands, handheld weapons clashing, and fallen soldiers uttering final cries. Colonel Prescott gave the order for all survivors to retreat through the rear exit of the redoubt. Men poured out as they attempted to escape to the safety of yonder Bunker Hill. Despite his best efforts, Prescott couldn't coax Joseph away from the chaos before the others. Joseph remained behind to ensure each one made it out before the oncoming redcoats could reach them. His final act of selflessness would cost him the ultimate price.

One of the final shots ringing out late that Saturday afternoon sent a shock wave through the provincial forces. A British bullet went through Joseph's skull while he stood a few yards from the same exit that granted other men new life. Various accounts[36] also describe Joseph's side being pierced with a sword or bayonet to ensure his part in the war would end that day. He stood in the gap between certain death and the safety of his countrymen. The bullet and beating intended for them became his to bear that full and fateful eve.

Having Breed's Hill under their heels, the British didn't pursue the provincials toward Bunker. Generals Howe and Gage knew this Pyrrhic victory had cost them dearly, and their pause at this location reinforced the strategic importance that Joseph and others had placed on the distant, higher hill. Also, both generals considered Joseph's life to be worth 500 colonial soldiers,[37,38] akin to the entire contingent of men contained in the redoubt that day.

The redcoats turned their attention to burying the dead in the quickest way possible. Their actions resembled the Roman soldiers of Pesach AD 30 when they sought to discard the detritus of human remains in the Hinnom Valley. The British had several reasons for doing this: (1) the oppressive heat would transform exposed cadavers into a nightmarish environment for the living, (2) the British had suffered the much larger fatality count and didn't want the besieged observers to begin keeping a tally, (3) they also didn't want the observers to catalogue the atrocity of what the king's soldiers had done to their fellow countrymen, and (4) they wanted to prevent provincials coming that night or the next morning to gather their deceased and make a greater visible show of the martyrs through large funerals and remembrance ceremonies that could incite more strife. With the provincial forces not possessing any cannons, Gage decided to occupy the eastern part of the Charlestown Peninsula as a forceful annexation of the besieged Boston situation. He hoped that strengthening the siege would cause the provincials to succumb to the pressure and come to their senses. After all, who in their right minds would dare to engage in a long war of attrition with His Majesty's armed forces and the ruling world power of the day?

As the sun set, British soldiers, who had transitioned from sabers to shovels, callously threw the battlefield bodies into shallow trenches. They tossed Joseph into a small grave along with a nearby fellow fighter, simply described as a farmer.[39]

He was hastily buried in a common grave
with other nondescript rebels.

Joseph—as president *pro tem* of the Provincial Congress, chair of the Committee of Safety, instigator of the Committee of Correspondence, and a reputed organizer of a resistance, backing it all up with rousing orations—was one of Governor-General Gage's top targets to take down along with Samuel Adams and John Hancock. Gage had to ensure it truly was the famous Dr. Joseph Warren who had fallen at Breed's Hill that day.

Thus, Joseph's corpse wouldn't be allowed to rest in peace; Gage ordered General Howe to confirm it was in fact Warren lying there. Howe employed the expertise of a Dr. John Jeffries,[40] a loyalist physician who had been a friend and colleague of Joseph. Soldiers exhumed the freshly covered body for Dr. Jeffries's examination. Wanting it to be a mistake, Jeffries lamented when he informed Howe that it was indeed Warren. The attending redcoats celebrated fiendishly at having killed the one who had caused them so much trouble. Observers noted that soldiers rummaged through his clothes for any valuables and stripped the body of his outer garments, including one particular covering, and took the Book of Psalms he carried.[41,42]

A coat caught their attention

Friends and foes that day made special mention of Joseph's clothing. Not intending to stand out, he still garnered attention like the Joseph of Genesis did when wearing the coat of many colors (Genesis 37:3). As he had come to the battle in midday, not having been there all night toiling in the dirt to build the redoubt, Joseph's attire was pristine—something to be expected of a prominent physician and provincial president. He wasn't soiled with the dust, dirt, and soot as the other patriot defenders were. But the true focal point was the soldiers' fascination with his waistcoat,[43,44,45] a silk-fringed work of art crafted by the skilled hands of one who loved Joseph, cared for the widower's four children, and awaited their wedding day. Her name was Mercy. Ms. Mercy Scollay would never marry.

Reminiscent of what occurred at Golgotha almost two thousand years prior, the soldiers divided his clothes and other articles. A soldier eventually auctioned the prized waistcoat in Boston.[46,47] Certain accounts emphasize that the treasured garment was of a blue hue.[48]

It was reported[49] that the British soldiers repeatedly dug up Joseph's remains to satisfy the curiosity of onlookers, and word of their utter disrespect and disregard eventually found its way to John Adams and the rest of the Congress. The news served as the ether to ignite the righteous indignation of the delegates from across the colonies and unified them in purpose and perspective more than any speech or polemic could have done. His death and mistreatment galvanized men of renown the following year to rely on Divine Providence and pledge their lives, fortunes, and sacred honor (last line of the Declaration of Independence) to the cause Joseph so greatly emulated and inked with his own blood on that first major battlefield.

The news about the Battle of Bunker Hill quickly spread and inspired young men to join the newly formed army and fight for a cause that was previously unimaginable—freedom from oppressive government rule in order to pursue life, liberty, and happiness. One of these was *Joseph* Plumb Martin, and his name would rise to prominence after his passing in similar yet distinct fashion to that of his namesake Josephus from the first century AD.

Instead of being a military commander from a prominent family like Josephus, Joseph Plumb Martin was a young man with no real promising prospects in life.[50] He was born in western Massachusetts, and his parents sent him to live with his grandparents in Connecticut, where he learned how to read and write—to the great benefit of our American heritage and posterity. Like Josephus, he closely documented the key facts and events of that period, providing historians a unique treasure trove of information about the enlisted soldier's perspective of the American Revolutionary War.[51] Also, Joseph Plumb Martin comes onto the scene shortly after the death of the protagonist (Joseph Warren) as Josephus did following the Passion of Christ.

From Joseph's memoir, *Private Yankee Doodle*, historians have the "only complete account"[52] of what life was like as a soldier in the

Continental Army. It describes the soldiers' resolve during the most arduous conditions and the results of their most valiant contributions. By methodically capturing eyewitness experiences as Josephus did, Joseph cemented the most comprehensive record of firsthand accounts of battles like Long Island, White Plains, Germantown, Monmouth, and the Siege of Yorktown. Also, because Joseph's 8th Connecticut Regiment (17th Continental Regiment) encamped at Valley Forge during the grueling winter of 1777–1778, subsequent generations better understand the personal sacrifices and methodical discipline required to lay the foundation for American victory. Today, the primary multiuse trail throughout Valley Forge National Historic Park is named in his honor.

The value of Joseph Plumb Martin's memoir is that it relays the perspective of the ordinary soldier, the obscure and often overlooked contributor to the war effort and American independence when compared to the writings and reflections of Washington, Jefferson, and others in prominent positions. Following a brief respite after his first tour of duty from June to December of 1776, Joseph reenlisted in April 1777 for the remainder of the war—what became known as "for the duration" by the five thousand or so volunteers who decided to serve faithfully to the conflict's conclusion.[53] They were mainly humble, working-class people without land ownership or other major property rights. In contrast to the colonial militias that were comprised of farmers, merchants, and other men of means, those who comprised the enlisted corps of the army were the unsung heroes. While outmatched and underequipped, they bore the bulk of battlefield engagements to defeat a world empire. And they did so not only in a unified manner as one army working with associated militias, but as one people—approximately 15 percent of the army's fighting force consisted of African Americans standing alongside their fellows, not segregated into special units by skin color.[54] But while operations and accomplishments of a new army are inspiring and intriguing, the postwar American populace wanted to move past the heartbreaking tragedies of war and the veterans who had so valiantly worn the uniform for the sake of their freedom.

It's easy to understand, through the lens of human nature, why those throughout the colonies were ready to minimize the army's accomplishments and instead focus on the feats of the Minutemen. Americans didn't want to place too many accolades or emphasis on a standing army given the inhabitants' distrust of a strong central government with armed forces at its disposal to enforce its will as the British had done. And with weak Articles of Confederation barely tying the new states together—much less on the ways and means aspects of taxes and funding—there was no appetite or avenue to provide pensions to those who had served and now bore the bodily burdens of war. The burgeoning American paradigm became: Praise and ensconce in effigy the Minutemen and militia—the rapid-action citizen-soldiers who return to regular life after the imminent danger has passed. Beware of an army that requires regular investment and remembrance when bones, and skin and sinew prematurely age the veteran due to constant and continuous service to cover those who remain safe at home.

And so Joseph Plumb Martin penned his eyewitness account of a "for the duration" foot soldier to give an eternal voice to his band of brothers who endured the hardships of war and the families who bore the sobering ramifications in never seeing their loved ones return from the distant fields they plowed with artillery, bayonets, and sabers. He captured for posterity the conditions and commitments of Continental Army soldiers so that one day a nation would recall and recommit resources for their care.

Like Joseph Warren, Joseph Plumb Martin was considered a Revolutionary War hero in the early 1800s but then was largely forgotten in the years leading up to the Civil War. He embodied the commitment to a cause greater than oneself or one's personal safety. Joseph Plumb Martin was the truest example of a working-class American fighting not to protect any land holdings or personal property but to stand between destruction and his fellow civilians.

———•———

He was the eighteenth century Josephus, writing for
the sake and understanding of his people.

———•———

A few weeks after the Battle of Bunker Hill, new boots stood on the ground near the Breed's Hill redoubt and Joseph Warren's unmarked grave. General George Washington, his staff, and the initial contingent of a rapidly forming Continental Army took in the scene of a hill scarred by death and the charred remains of what had once been Charlestown. The British were currently not present at the hard-to-defend area, seeking instead to double down on the Boston siege and port stranglehold.

General Washington listened to the accounts of those who had fought alongside Joseph Warren as they relayed his final actions and selfless courage. It's been said that Washington was visibly moved upon learning of Warren's sacrifice and that the future first president considered Joseph the country's original commander in chief.[55]

The same day of the Bunker Hill battle, newly-appointed General Washington and his nascent forces had departed Philadelphia for Massachusetts.[56] On July 3, 1775—one year and a day before the future nation's declared birthdate—Washington consolidated overall command[57] of all militias and other fighting forces in the Cambridge and Charlestown Peninsula arena as Warren had so patiently and persistently advocated for.

Warren's consistent clarion call for colonial unity was further realized when Georgia convened its Provincial Congress in Savannah the following day—July 4, 1775—to endorse the Continental Congress in Philadelphia, designate delegates, and adopt the trade ban against Britain.[58] It was the final segment of Franklin's "Join, or Die" metaphor and the thirteenth rattle of resolute warning on Gadsden's coiled serpent standard. Similar to what occurred in Jerusalem following the death of One on a hill near the city's outskirts, people began to truly unify for a cause beyond their wildest imaginations in the weeks and months following Joseph's death.

The passing of night
gives way to dawn's light
as from the east the sun's glory approaches.

It rises to greet
men gathered to meet
warm rays brought by heaven's horsemen and coaches.

What have they wrought
after battles were fought
on bloody fields and desks of committee.

A new republic to build
by every tradesman and guild
so all could see, what it means, to be free.

CHAPTER EIGHT

A RISING SUN AND
A WAXING MOON

Breed's Hill, outskirts of Charlestown | March 17, 1776 | John 12:24

When death leads to birth, like a seed in the earth.

I T WAS NINE MONTHS TO THE DAY SINCE THE BATTLE OF BUNKER
Hill—the same time frame as the gestation period for human life. On
this near-spring Sunday, as sunrise greeted this first day of the week, the
hillside was awash in warm, celestial rays. Soon, John[1] and others would
rush to locate an unmarked hillside tomb. They are able to approach
the area because the empire's soldiers were no longer posted near the
site. The siege on the city had been broken. The occupation was over.
The stranglehold had ended.

Not much had transpired in Boston and its environs for the remainder
of 1775 following the battle and consolidation by both sides. It was a
summer through winter solstice stalemate.

General Washington used those months to build the army,
formulate supply lines, and prepare for the collisions that 1776 promised
to bring. He also waited for the cannons from Fort Ticonderoga that
Benedict Arnold originally intended to deliver. Arnold, along with
Ethan Allen and the Green Mountain Boys (of the later Vermont

Republic), had successfully captured the fort in a dawn surprise attack on May 10, 1775—more than a month before the Bunker Hill battle—but Arnold was hampered by numerous challenges related to conflicts in command and a lack of resources to move the massive guns.[2] This internal bickering and disunity by the victorious rebel forces was one of the first instances of frustration that inserted a seed of bitterness, which later turned his heart toward switching sides.

Knowing this heavy artillery was needed to break Britain's siege of Boston, General Washington dispatched Henry Knox in December 1775 to go retrieve them. Knox returned with the cannons the following month (late January 1776) in what is regarded as one of the most impressive logistical feats of the war. What Warren and Arnold had initiated and conceived, Washington and Knox completed and received.[3]

Possessing the cannons, Washington commemorated the sixth anniversary of the Boston Massacre of March 5, 1770, by moving the heavy artillery into position on Dorchester Heights,[4] an elevated portion of land strategically situated south-southeast of the city. When the British realized the extent of firepower aimed at them, His Majesty's forces, along with many loyalists, loaded the ships within two weeks and evacuated the city. With British boots and muskets nowhere near Breed's Hill, Joseph Warren's family and friends could safely search the site for his remains in the hopes of providing a proper burial.

Joseph's brothers, Dr. John "Jack" Warren and Ebenezer "Eben,"[5] headed to the hill with the arduous task of locating a nondescript, nine-month-old shallow grave and then dealing with the sight of what natural processes had done to the clay composition of their loved one. They were likely joined by Paul Revere and other Masonic members.

Paul and Joseph were the dearest of friends throughout the years leading up to the war that raged around them. They had grieved together upon losing their wives to natural causes within a two-week period in the spring of 1773.[6] Now Paul would have to say goodbye to Joseph as well.

Paul, as a silversmith, also was the best one to identify the skull. Part of his trade was prosthetic dentistry, and he had fitted and fastened two ivory teeth with silver wire in Joseph's mouth[7,8] not long before the battles of 1775 ensued.

Carefully searching the hill since March 21, the men didn't locate Joseph until Thursday, April 4.[9] In 1776, April 4 also was the Hebrew holy day of Pesach (Passover). They carried his remains to the State House at the head of State Street, where his coffin was on display for three days. This Passover weekend coincided with Easter (formerly Eostre) and the three days of Jesus lying in Joseph of Arimathea's tomb.

As the Warren family didn't own a burial plot in Boston, Judge George Richards Minot, a family friend, offered the temporary use of his grave site in the Granary Burying Ground.[10,11,12] It is where other famous Sons of Liberty—Samuel Adams, John Hancock, Robert Treat Paine, and Paul Revere—joined Joseph after their earthly assignments and journeys were complete. On Monday, April 8, 1776, family and friends carefully placed Joseph in the Minot family plot and tearfully relayed their farewells.

He died on a hill among common men and received
a temporary burial in a rich man's tomb.

Joseph didn't remain at the Granary cemetery. In fact, he was moved more than any other Founder. Before John Adams died in 1826, Joseph already had undergone three burials. His fifth and final placement occurred August 8, 1856, at the Forest Hills Cemetery in Roxbury, Massachusetts[13]—the town of his origin. The movement of his bones with respect to that of the nation's other patriarchs is unique—like that of the Joseph of Genesis.

And Moses took the bones of Joseph with him,
for he had placed the children of Israel under solemn oath, saying,

"God will surely visit you, and you shall carry
up my bones from here with you."
—*Exodus 13:19*

———•———

At the conclusion of the Book of Joshua—the book of
conflict and conquest—the burials of Joseph and Joshua, in
the land of origination and inheritance, are emphasized.

The bones of Joseph, which the children of
Israel had brought up out of Egypt,
they buried at Shechem, in the plot of ground which Jacob had bought
from the sons of Hamor the father of Shechem
for one hundred pieces of silver,
and which had become an inheritance of the children of Joseph.
—*Joshua 24:32*

———•———

Midway between Joseph's lying in state and the issuance of the
Declaration of Independence was Shavuot or the Feast of Weeks
(late May that year). In AD 30, Shavuot was the nexus of a major
movement—the birth of the church and ultimate liberty. In 1776, it
was the philosophical fulcrum of a similar yet secular message of unity
and freedom, which itself still resonates around the globe.

Between early April and early July, there was a flurry of activity in
the colonies and the Continental Congress. The Congress could not
declare independence from Britain as it was simply a structure of gathering
delegates from thirteen autonomous governments. What this confederation
required was for a majority of the colonial councils or provincial congresses
to authorize their delegates to discuss and vote on such an audacious
measure. Also, the delegates from at least one colony would have to come
with specific instructions of proposing such a declaration to the larger
body. And whichever colony proffered such a treasonous act was sure to
receive the full attention and wrath of His Majesty's forces.

Although Massachusetts had been the flagship of rebellion against Parliament's heavy hand, the first colony to act upon the idea of actual independence was North Carolina. On April 12, 1776, it passed the Halifax Resolves,[14] which authorized its delegates to vote for independence if such a resolution was introduced by another colony. This date of decisiveness is prominently shown on the bottom left of the current state flag.

On May 15, John Adams's preamble for a resolution to declare independence was approved by the Congress. On the same day, the Virginia Convention unanimously voted to have its delegates go to the Congress and introduce the motion to dissolve colonial allegiance to Great Britain and become free and independent states.[15] This motion materialized within the walls of Independence Hall on June 7 when Virginia's senior delegate, Richard Henry Lee, presented the resolution to the Continental Congress. It led to the creation of a five-member committee to draft a declaration of independence. In less than a month, on July 4, 1776, Congress voted on and approved the document penned by Thomas Jefferson that still inspires millions today as the cornerstone of a nation's foundation and of a brave people fighting to be free.

The Upper Room, Jerusalem | just prior to Shavuot
or the Feast of Weeks/Pentecost | AD 30[16]
Acts 1:15–2:1
Baptism by fire.

In the days immediately following what Peter and the other apostles had witnessed on the Mount of Olives, they continued to gather in the Upper Room with a large group of disciples, including Jesus's mother Mary and others who had followed and supported the Messiah during His mortal sojourn on earth as the Son of Man. They were waiting for the fulfillment of the promise of being baptized with power from on high, and all they knew to do was obey the instruction to wait, watch, and pray.

As they did so, Peter felt compelled to fill the gap caused by Judas Iscariot's betrayal and death. While the glaring vacancy would seem to have been the absence of their Master, Teacher, Rabbi, Healer, Mentor, Provider, Savior, and Friend, they placed a special emphasis on reestablishing the order of twelve apostles.

Twelve wasn't just an arbitrary number; it reflected a pattern that reinforced the principle of pairs as first exhibited with the creatures on the ark. It also showed that these founders of the faith were focused on the future while remembering and restoring the patterns of the past:

- The pattern of twelve apostles walking along the shores of the Sea of Galilee while listening to the voice that even schools of fish would heed when beckoned from the depths into awaiting nets.

- The pattern of twelve sons of Jacob that would become twelve tribes of a nation like no other.

- The pattern of the promise of twelve princes out of Ishmael, the son Abraham watched fade into the distance until the horizon enveloped him.

- The pattern of twelve hours of light to delineate a day, and an opposite twelve hours of varying degrees of darkness to designate a night.

- The pattern of twelve months measured by each orbit of the moon around the earth while the earth completes its cycle around the sun.

- The pattern of twelve years for Jupiter, the king planet, to accomplish its heliocentric course and return to its original position on the starlit stage.

So twelve is about the completion of a cycle, the establishment of organized authority, and the orchestrated art of timing. Timing that marks development and achievement—Jesus at age twelve teaching in the temple; the timing of enduring a season of life—the woman with the issue of blood for twelve years who touched the hem of His garment (Matthew 9:20–21); and the choreographed timing of each year's four seasons and the heavenly signs that continue like clockwork on a set pattern (Genesis 8:22; Isaiah 40:26).

Understanding the importance of the pattern, the apostles handled Judas's replacement with extreme care and fervent prayer. In addition to the twelve apostles during Jesus's earthly ministry, He also had a group of seventy disciples who followed Him (Luke 10:1, 17; Acts 1:21–22). A majority of them, if not all, probably were part of the 120 mentioned in Acts 1:15.

From this gathering, the apostles selected two men. They didn't just quickly pick a substitute; they cautiously called two divinely appointed candidates for consideration. The next step was crucial as they were determined to build cohesion and consensus during this critical time. Their entire world had changed over the past fifty days, and they were intent on weaving a tight tapestry of teamwork—a first-century band of brothers. The one they selected would be handed the opportunity to either help synchronize their efforts or sabotage their endeavors.

It marks the only time in scripture that this type of selection process was employed in which two positive candidates were singled out, but only one was selected.*** There was a similar incident in Acts 6 when the apostles asked the larger group of disciples to select seven men to serve as deacons, but it doesn't mention them creating a list of specific individuals and then culling the candidates to the prescribed number. Which raises the question: Why didn't the eleven apostles discuss and pray among themselves and *then* pick a promising individual from the group? That method would have negated any embarrassment and potential backlash from the one who wasn't chosen.

*** Note: Throughout the Old Testament, there are similar yet distinctly different instances from the Acts account of casting lots to select between two creatures (the goats in Leviticus 16:8; Saul and Jonathan in 1 Samuel 14:42), to find the culprit (Jonah 1:7), and to determine the placement and/or timing of duties (1 Chronicles 24:31; 25:8; 26:13–14; Nehemiah 10:34; 11:1).

With respect to human frailty and humiliation, recall that the apostles had argued among themselves during their days with Jesus about who would be the greatest (Matthew 18:1; Mark 9:33–34; Luke 9:46; 22:24).

Even the mother of James and John took it upon herself to ask Jesus for her two sons to be enthroned next to Him (Matthew 20:20–24). Human pride and self-preservation often cause people to unwittingly seek promotion and strategic location to protect and pad the ego. Sometimes ignorantly and other times intentionally, they try inserting their "rightful place" mantra into the equation. Jesus made a point of doing the opposite when invited to sit at a banquet—choose the lowliest seat so as to be promoted to a better spot instead of clamoring for the prime seat and being demoted to a lesser location and thus humiliated in front of all those gathered around the table (Luke 14:7–11).

With this in mind, imagine the feeling of disappointment and disgust a disciple would experience when called to stand up for possible selection and elevation, only to be told "Never mind" and made to sit back down in front of everyone—and recorded in scripture for millions to see as the one passed over for a promotion. This awkward experience happened to a man named Joseph, and ironically, it was how he reacted to the situation that was the key and catalyst to strength and unity.

The two men identified for consideration on the eve of Shavuot were Matthias and Joseph, often referred to as Barsabas, with the surname of Justus (Acts 1:23). While the Bible and Western Asia (aka Middle Eastern) cultures place a very high value on the giving and meaning of names, there are only a handful of instances in the Bible where multiple labels for one person are mentioned with such a pause for emphasis as happens here. With the name Joseph referring to increase and exponential addition or multiplication, it is usually a very positive connotation.

The title of Barsabas (Barsabbas in various biblical versions) is only used twice in scripture, both occurring in the book of Acts. The term could be patronymic, meaning it is related to a father's name, as "bar" is the Aramaic form of the Hebrew word "ben," which means "son of." Therefore, it would be describing this Joseph as a son of Sabas or Sabba (Yosef Bar-Sabba in Hebrew).[17] Recall that there was a highly esteemed disciple named Judas Barsabas in Acts 15:22 who went with Silas, Paul, and Barnabas to Antioch for apostolic work. From the patronymic perspective, many scholars consider these two men (Joseph and Judas) to be brothers, which would put Joseph in good company in terms of Christian pedigree.

Other schools of thought view the Barsabas term not as familial but as a title denoting commendable qualities, as it could mean "son of an elder," "old man," "grandfather," "wisdom," "fulfillment," "satisfaction," "completion," or "sabbath."[18] From that standpoint, this Joseph candidate was one of renowned character and sound judgment—a peacemaker and sage—traits the early church would need when getting established and beginning to grow.

The character aspect is prominently pronounced with the third moniker of Justus. Unlike the first two titles for this man, the third is not Hebrew-oriented but denotes a Greek or Latin aspect. So not only was this Joseph well-respected by the Jewish community, but he had a worthy reputation in the Gentile or Roman realm as well. This type of standing in the secular community was a point that Paul stressed to Timothy about the qualities of a bishop in 1 Timothy 3:7. The Justus title reflected justice, integrity, and a particularly high level of righteousness or holiness.[19] Jesus's brother James, a leader of the church in Jerusalem, was similarly called James the Just. The title also is associated with two other devout men—one whom Paul lodged with in Acts 18, and a fellow worker and comforting friend to Paul in Colossians 4.

Understanding the names and traits associated with this Joseph, and with the name Matthias, meaning "the gift of Jah/God,"[20] the apostles had undoubtedly performed due diligence in focusing their attention on these two men. Whatever was to come out of the next few moments when the apostles cast their lots was left to the x-ray inspection of the Almighty, for God looks past names, postures, and pedigrees to the heart and soul of the selectee.

When the last verse of Acts 1 relays that the lot fell on Matthias as the right choice, many people, both the ignorant and the astute, move on to Acts 2 thinking Joseph was lacking in some way. Knowing that no human is perfect, they are partially correct, but mostly incorrect if that is the final summation of the matter as almost every human possesses positive and still-under-construction or should-be-discarded attributes. The primary fault in the calculations is the presumption that there was a flaw in Joseph's heart that tipped the scales in God choosing Matthias as the better person.

Rather, could it be that both men had attributes suited for *that* moment on *that* day? Maybe, just maybe the one selected to join the ranks of the high-profile apostles mainly was there to fill a gap while the other possessed a wealth of humility and wisdom to be passed over for promotion and serve with the same enthusiasm and passion anyway. Nothing against Matthias, but along with Joseph, he is mentioned in Acts 1 for the first and last time in the scriptures.

The secret ingredient in the situation wasn't one man being better than the other; it was the combination of the two working together in various realms and roles to help bring forth a miracle when "the Day of Pentecost had fully come" (Acts 2:1). Reflect upon the lineage of Jesus described in Luke 3 where there are several fathers with some version of the name Matthias or Joseph, significantly more mentions than any other titles throughout that royal genealogy. And remember Leah, the great matriarch, when she arrived at the point of not focusing on her shadowed situation but instead gave intrinsic meaning to the name of Judah and initiated this lineage of mighty men.

———•———

The beginning of Acts 2—the chapter in the Bible
when the Holy Spirit explodes onto the stage,
fills the house, and ignites the birth of the church—shows how
the atmosphere was accentuated by Joseph's reaction.

———•———

They were all with one accord in one place.
—Acts 2:1

———•———

Joseph didn't murmur, initiate a protest, or stage a walkout. His childlike faith and humble perspective—admirable qualities emphasized by Jesus in Matthew 18:2–4—set the example and gave life to greater obedience and servanthood among the believers. Like Revolutionary War foot soldier Joseph Plumb Martin, Joseph Barsabas Justus served faithfully in his initial nondescript place to foster a cause the entire world would soon appreciate. This disciple helped set the Upper Room altar environment in order for heavenly fire to fall, and in doing so, the fire fell upon him in the same manner ... and with the same power ... as upon those of the inner circle.

Extrabiblical accounts and legends mention a man called Justus becoming a bishop in the area of Betaris, later known as Eleutheropolis. Flavius Josephus describes its destruction by Vespasian in AD 68 during the Jewish uprising and resultant wars with the Roman empire.[21] Rebuilt and reestablished by the Romans around AD 200, it was given the Greek name Eleutheropolis[22] to denote a free city as its inhabitants were exempt from certain taxes and enjoyed varying degrees of autonomy compared to that of the surrounding area.[23] Today, it sits in Israel's Beit Guvrin-Maresha National Park, with Beit Guvrin being associated with the Betaris/Eleutheropolis site. The Beit Guvrin name is derived from the ancient Aramaic title of Beth Gabra, meaning "the house of strong men"[24] or the house of the powerful people. Therefore, if Joseph Barsabas Justus did migrate from Jerusalem to this site after the Acts 2 account, then he would have been a key figure in an area of the Holy Land that later became known as the land of the free and the home of the brave.

———

Independence Hall, Philadelphia, Pennsylvania | September 17, 1787
Days of Awe, Introspection, and Inspiration.

The war had been over for four years and two weeks, and Dr. Joseph Warren had been killed in action *twelve* years ago. The men who were gathered remembered his words and ultimate sacrifice, as that of many others, on this special day. Independence Hall (then known as the old

Pennsylvania State House) again contained delegates who had come together from across the colonies, now called commonwealths and states, to finalize and sign another momentous document. Joseph had helped inspire and instigate the words and warrants of the Declaration of Independence eleven years prior, and his memory now moved the pen strokes of this second major assembly of signers.

It had been twelve years since the lighting of the two lanterns shining across the Charles River and a waning moon's odd placement against a blinded man-of-war. Twelve years since the restless shadows around Boston Common and the gilded weathercock bathed in moonlight as Revere arrived in Lexington. A twelve-year season of bloody battlefields and human determination to see a land finally restored and healed. A twelve-year cycle of colonies choosing to unite in order to produce new life. After the taxes, the tea, the tempest, and the trials, now a convention of coming together to take the next step toward a more perfect union.

The interim Articles of Confederation were too weak and ineffective in striking the right balance between state sovereignty and national unity. George Washington, the former commanding general whom Joseph had originally advocated for, led the Continental Army to victory and now presided over this "Grand Convention at Philadelphia."[25] It wasn't known as the Constitutional Convention until later, as the original intent of the delegates was to fix the existing Articles, not replace them with a completely different document. The gathering evolved into a three and a half month marathon of heated arguments mixed with calculated conversations, similar in scope and significance to that of the Second Continental Congress during the Declaration discussions.

The convention originally was set to begin on May 14, but only a few delegates had arrived by that time. On Friday, May 25, they were able to begin when representatives from seven states were present to secure a quorum. Rhode Island never sent any delegates, so the convention consisted of *twelve* participating states. They had not planned the timing this way, but the proceedings commenced immediately following Shavuot (the Feast of Weeks/Pentecost) that year. From their perspective, it was a twelve-day delay. Following a different calendar, it was exactly on time.

Their work through the stifling summer of closed-door debates and deliberations produced the construct of a republic that has survived for nearly 250 years. This assembly produced the original 4,400-word, four-page document[26] that became the new nation's blueprint for a balanced government, with power split among three branches and with significant say and sovereignty resting with the people in their several states.

And now the moment was upon them. As the autumn season approached, the delegates likely were not aware that they were concluding the convention literally in a new era. On a calendar invisible to most but consequential nonetheless, the delegates lined up to sign the Constitution of the United States in the middle of the Days of Awe— the period between Rosh Hashanah (the beginning of the Hebrew civil year) and Yom Kippur (the Day of Atonement). This ten-day period is considered by many to be the holiest time on the biblical calendar.[27]

With Rosh Hashanah being the only day set in Leviticus that is marked by a new moon, the creation of the Constitution occurred during a waxing (increasing) moon phase compared to the waning moon of Revere's midnight ride. And like the moon's role in the darkness of night, this new United States of America would begin to dissipate the gloom of human governments by reflecting a greater Light. Sometimes she doesn't shine as brightly or majestically as desired—depending on her position relative to the sun and earth (the Light and the world), but this nation still has the capacity to serve as an illuminating beacon and a shining city on a hill.

Franklin's focus transitions from a serpent to the sun

Being advanced in age and several years senior to the other delegates in the room, Benjamin Franklin was the esteemed grandfather of the Founders. As he saw his 1754 admonition of "Join, or Die" finally fulfilled, Dr. Franklin addressed the group one last time as delegates waited their turn to sign the document. In his remarks, he made a point of touching upon the sun painted on the top of the chair George Washington used throughout the proceedings. He noted that artists had a difficult time painting a sun's phase in terms of displaying whether it was rising or setting. Benjamin Franklin recounted to the listeners that, throughout the summer sessions of interstate arguments and political posturing, he had sat and reflected upon whether that sun was meant to relay a rising or setting condition for the country. As the delegates had reached an amenable consensus on this new constitution and striving for *e pluribus unum*, Franklin concluded that he was pleased to see it was, in fact, a rising sun.[28]

INDEPENDENCE HALL ASSEMBLY ROOM. SOURCE: AUTHOR'S PERSONAL PHOTOGRAPH.

THE PAINTED SUN AT THE TOP OF THE CHAIRPERSON'S SEAT. SOURCE: AUTHOR'S PERSONAL PHOTOGRAPH.

One of the three men present that day who didn't line up to sign the document was Elbridge Gerry—the close friend of Joseph Warren and co-laborer on the Massachusetts Provincial Congress in the days leading up to the war. It was he who had spent the most time with Joseph during those fatal forty-eight hours before the battle on Breed's Hill. Future Congressman, governor, and then vice president, Gerry didn't readily endorse the new constitution until it included a Bill of Rights to guarantee it was the people, not the states or a new central government, who were the focal point in both the spirit and letter of the law.

Looking across the room that day was a poignant moment for Elbridge. His dear friend Joseph was gone, and their other esteemed Sons of Liberty brethren were elsewhere—Samuel Adams, John Hancock, and Paul Revere attending to other matters in Massachusetts and John Adams in England. Even the Virginian Thomas Jefferson couldn't take in the scene due to his diplomatic duties in France. They had come so far, sacrificed so much, and yet there was a lifetime's worth of work waiting on them still. The task before them: build a new nation, eradicate the scourge of slavery, and truly become a beacon on a hill.

———•———

If twenty-first-century America is in her waning moon phase,
then let it be the time of lantern lighting
triggered by Warren-type watchmen
and the itinerant riding of Reveres, Daweses, and
Prescotts to ignite the gunpowder of prayer.

———•———

It's not a sunset but a genesis moment of new Josephs
in a world faced with the lean cattle of pestilence
and the pernicious stalks of pandemic.
It's a moment requiring those who understand
the times and can interpret dreams
to relay the proper prophetic pronouncements of the day.

———•———

And what does the LORD require of you
But to do justly,
To love mercy,
And to walk humbly with your God?
—Micah 6:8

EPILOGUE

The age-old and elementary axiom that
2 + 2 = 4 is true, but it's not automatic.
The basic form can be deceiving.

It all depends on the use of the decimal, and
what follows to the right of it.
For those who oversimplify the equation, it could
lead to an Orwellian 2 + 2 equaling 5.

There has to be a decimal—a point of definitive
demarcation—to identify the significant figures.
And what sits behind the scene (off to the
right) has to remain small—
still very significant, but small in the
quantitative or magnitude realm.

If anything greater than two (2) exists behind the invisible decimal,
then the rounding rule would create a five (5).
Example: 2.3 + 2.3 = 4.6, thus 5.

The placement and interaction of significant figures is especially true
in the arena of expanse and escalation because
imprecise measurements, when magnified,
lead to massive miscalculations.

And such miscalculations—when coupled
with an increase in power, position,
responsibility, and influence—can have devastating ramifications.

The basic component (the number 2) of math's
simple axiom (2 + 2 = 4) is also profound.
It is the only number that serves as the nexus
between addition and multiplication,
between natural progression and exponential expansion.

It is the only even prime number in existence,
and denotes pairing, coupling, and unity.
It is the only digit, besides the nothingness of zero (0), that,
when either added or multiplied by itself, produces the same outcome.

It creates a single point on the graph (*x marks the spot*) before
the paths of simple addition and exponential multiplication
diverge in drastic fashion after just a few iterations.

One trajectory increases at a steady pace
while the other path begins accelerating skyward.

In the Joseph domain of "*let him add, he shall
increase (exponentially as in **multiply**),*"
all aspects of the equation have to be correct to align
with proper waypoints as the speed of the situation surges
and the stress of environmental factors escalates.

In transitioning from 2 + 2 = 4 to 2 x 2 = 4, the
sole significant figure behind the decimal
can't be larger than one (1) to retain the equation's consistency.

A two (2) behind the decimal, which worked in simple addition,
would cause the rounding rule in 2 x 2 to
again equal an erroneous five (5).
Example: 2.**2** x 2.**2** = 4.84, thus 5.

Therefore, to maintain the integrity of the 2 + 2 = 4 and
2 x 2 = 4 nexus, the significant figure variable to the right of the
decimal can't be greater than one (1)—the lowest whole number.

The least shall be the greatest (Matthew 2:6;
11:11; Luke 7:28; 9:48; Ephesians 3:8).

Enoch (in Genesis) experienced this phenomenon as
the first to be translated and not see death because he
understood the transformational power of humility and
focusing outwardly toward God and others, as Leah had learned.
He went from being a one (1) in the decimal realm to a zero (0),
and melted into the essence of the equation
and into the realm of the eternal.

"And Enoch walked with God; and he was not,
for God took him" (Genesis 5:24).
Don't be deceived by the simple form of things. Remember that
what appears small and behind the decimal really has the greatest
force in keeping the numbers and subsequent calculations in
check and aligned with distant destinations and designations.

Therefore:
The smallest, yet extremely significant, figure that
sits behind the decimal makes the difference.

———•———

As Joseph Warren proceeded through life and increased in position and
prominence, this significant figure trended toward the zero behind the
decimal. While he was out in front of the action in many ways and a
primary part of the core Sons of Liberty group, his most important
work was behind the scenes and in the shadows of the men who would
survive him and carry the work forward.

Though most of his writing in the public realm was either through
the use of pseudonyms or the consensus of a committee, his personalized

letters revealed his disposition. To whomever he would address his correspondence, he would conclude the message with a message all its own. The space right before he penned his name would resonate with some form of the phrase "your servant"[1] that would show the bearing of his life's course heading. On June 16, 1775, the day before his death, Joseph—as president of the Provincial Congress and thus the highest rank in the land—wrote a note to a military commander as they made final preparations for the following day's engagements. The brief yet broad memo ended with a zero-behind-the-decimal statement: "your most obedient, humble servant."[2]

In the heat of the battle, Joseph didn't seek the safety of a major general's perch, but went to the trenches to endure the bombardment with those of lowest rank. In between the deadly volleys, he didn't take a break to reload or regain his composure but went throughout the redoubt in an attempt to aid the wounded and the dying. He didn't wave an ensign above the fort to rally the men; he *was* the distinguished emblem in action.

———•———

So how is it that this pre-American emblem and icon of icons could be forgotten and become a mere footnote in whatever school textbooks relay about *actual* Revolutionary War history?

It seems that those who are called Joseph have a proclivity for being disregarded over time. The trend begins in Genesis with Pharaoh's butler forgetting the young man who interpreted the dream that restored him to good standing with the head of the Egyptian dynasty.

"Yet the chief butler did not remember Joseph,
but forgot him" (Genesis 40:23).

This first instance might seem plausible given that, at the time, Joseph was a nondescript prisoner—more of a number than a name, a Hebrew to be eschewed rather than an Egyptian to be elevated. What creates the enigmatic anomaly is that it happens again, to a much larger degree, by an entire empire and its people, after he had saved them from starvation and utter ruin. Perhaps it was due to a pharaoh from a new dynasty erasing most of the previous administration's records and accomplishments, in an ancient form of rewriting history to match the mentality and worldview of the new ruling class.

"Now there arose a new king over Egypt, who
did not know Joseph" (Exodus 1:8).

As the American War of Independence continued, Joseph Warren's colleagues and Masonic brethren ensured his name was enshrined far and wide. One of the initial monuments commemorating a Revolutionary War event, and thus one of the first public memorials erected in the later United States, was in 1797 on the Breed's Hill battlefield.[3] The Warren label also was affixed to many places and things up through the mid-nineteenth century. There are *twelve* states that have a county bearing this moniker, including some in the antebellum South and even extending into the Midwest. Besides counties, numerous other locations and public infrastructure carry his name, whether they are cities, streets, bridges, buildings, or five US Navy ships.[4]

It's as if Joseph's fame happened too soon and too suddenly as the timing and subsequent trends worked contrary to his national legacy. His death at the beginning of the war prevented further accounts of heroic exploits throughout the nine-year conflict and any prominent positions he might hold as a victor, similar to the acclaim George Washington received. This absence, coupled with a significant portion of his writings being destroyed in a fire,[5] means historians have little to work with compared to the libraries' worth of material from others of that era (e.g., Washington, John Adams, Thomas Jefferson, and Benjamin Franklin).

Following Joseph's death, General Benedict Arnold worked with Samuel Adams and John Hancock in securing financial support for their friend's four orphaned children. With Joseph and Benedict being close associates during the initial stages of the war, their kinship gave each other strength and solace as they prepared to confront the British lion. Benedict Arnold didn't defect to the British side until five years after Joseph's passing, but his name becoming synonymous with high treason in American parlance tarnished Joseph's legacy through the stigma of guilt by association.

Joseph Warren's views on all people truly being created equal—not just as a phrase to elicit awe on a declaration—fell out of fashion, as slavery drove the South's economic engines and settlers viewed Native Americans as a nuisance to new frontiers. Joseph's words from his March 5, 1772, commemoration of the Boston Massacre still resonated in their collective consciences when he reflected upon Native Americans being the first and "rightful proprietors"[6] of the land and how he embodied the ethos that Crispus Attucks (of African descent) was a fellow human being cut down by British aggression.

As northern and southern states grew more polarized on the eve of the Civil War, many Southerners wanted to overlook the fact that those who fought side by side in the April, May, and June 1775 battles were men with a variety of skin colors working together toward the same objective. Joseph Warren's legacy was an uncomfortable reminder of that fact. Focusing on the heroics of Virginia plantation owners Washington and Jefferson was a little more palatable.

Finally, the nation's memory of Joseph was further fragmented as northern and southern states began pulling apart. Originally epitomized by all Americans as the prominent proponent of national unity and sacrificing for the sake of others, Warren was gradually eschewed by Southerners as the idea of strengthening the unity of the Republic became not only taboo but anathema. At the same time, Henry Wadsworth Longfellow's 1860 poem about Paul Revere's ride to warn the countryside placed Revere in the limelight without any mention of Joseph's larger role.[7] It appears that Joseph's contributions to the Revolutionary War effort were undermined by the Civil War's strife.

Even in the midst of the Civil War's anguish and affliction, there were Joseph-type leaders like Colonel Joshua Chamberlain to help turn the tide. When others watched and wondered, he took decisive action ... and altered the arc of human history.[8] It's amazing how one life can so drastically affect things. And yet, knowing the importance of each person and his or her intrinsic worth, it shouldn't be so surprising but more commonly appreciated.

———•———

Only in recent decades has the story of Joseph Warren begun to reemerge. In his January 20, 1981, inaugural address, President Ronald Reagan reawakened this awareness. He mentioned Dr. Joseph Warren as "one of the greatest among the Founding Fathers"[9] and quoted an admonition to his compatriots that remains applicable to those living in succeeding centuries.

> "On you depend the fortunes of America. You are to decide the important question, on which rest the happiness and liberty of millions yet unborn. Act worthy of yourselves."[10,11]

> So walk in accordance with your calling, and "walk worthy of the calling with which you were called" (Ephesians 4:1).

———•———

Dr. Joseph Warren didn't seek position or prominence; he chose a supporting role of purpose so that others could take center stage. Our aim should not be just to admire but to emulate his characteristics and qualities—to activate that which has been incubated within us to lead, support, and inspire when others hesitate.

Now you know his name and just some of his story. May you find your center-stage or supporting role and live it to the fullest. You're not here in time or space by accident; rather, your life has unique and ultimate purpose.

Just as Longfellow's poem propelled Paul Revere to prominence, hopefully this alliterative prose produces a similar result in honor of Joseph Warren and the Josephs of old who preceded him in preparing the path and pattern. But moreover, may you be even more inspired and intent on living a life of servant leadership. The lives and liberties of others will benefit from it, and your anonymous actions will produce unanimous benefits to many you will never meet—while here on earth.

Respond to all your cues, proactively create opportunities for others, and fulfill your part of a story that is much larger than your extended sphere of influence.

Ask the right questions.
Walk boldly to the threshold.
Proceed circumspectly through the door.
Pivot to the purpose that truly matters.
Fill in the gaps, and turn mountains into molehills.
Sign up to serve "for the duration," and then
see it through to the conclusion.

The Josephs in that great cloud of witnesses salute you.
May your anointing and election be true in clearly
seeing and understanding every clue.

2.0

Having been forgotten and overlooked by most of his countrymen for the past 160 years, perhaps the 250th anniversaries of April 19 and June 17 (in 2025) will restore Joseph Warren to his place of proper recognition and credit for his role in precipitating independence.

And in Joseph Warren's habit of uttering a Latin phrase
to capture the essence of the moment and what lay ahead,
may you *carpe diem* (seize the day),
for tomorrow is a projection, not a promise.

CARPE DIEM

NOTES

CHAPTER ONE – TEA AND A TIMBER RATTLESNAKE

1   Samuel A. Forman, *Dr. Joseph Warren: The Boston Tea Party, Bunker Hill, and the Birth of American Liberty* (Gretna, LA: Pelican Publishing, 2012), 54.
2   History.com Editors, "Townshend Acts," A&E Television Networks, November 9, 2009, https://www.history.com/topics/american-revolution/townshend-acts.
3   Richard Frothingham, *Life and Times of Joseph Warren* (Whitefish, MT: Kessinger, 2007), 234.
4   Janet Uhlar, *Liberty's Martyr* (Indianapolis, IN: Dog Ear Publishing, 2009), 51.
5   Uhlar, 62.
6   Forman, *Dr. Joseph Warren*, 114.
7   Uhlar, *Liberty's Martyr*, 99.
8   Matthew 16:18.
9   Forman, *Dr. Joseph Warren*, 171–172.
10 Forman, 172.
11 Frothingham, *Life and Times of Joseph Warren*, 249.
12 Forman, *Dr. Joseph Warren*, 173.
13 Ibid.
14 Frothingham, *Life and Times of Joseph Warren*, 274.
15 Forman, *Dr. Joseph Warren*, 166.
16 Forman, 176.
17 Bob Ruppert, "The Rattle Snake Tells the Story," *Journal of the American Revolution*, January 14, 2015, https://allthingsliberty.com/2015/01/the-rattlesnake-tells-the-story/.
18 Ibid.
19 Benjamin Franklin, *Join or Die*, United States, May 9, 1754, [Photograph], Library of Congress, https://www.loc.gov/item/2002695523/.

20 Forman, *Dr. Joseph Warren*, 177.

21 Ibid.

22 Ibid.

23 Uhlar, *Liberty's Martyr*, 33.

24 Frothingham, *Life and Times of Joseph Warren*, 150.

25 Donald W. Olson and Russell L. Doescher, "Astronomical Computing: Paul Revere's Midnight Ride," *Sky and Telescope*, April 1992: 437–40.

26 Jacques Vialle and Darrel Hoff, "The Astronomy of Paul Revere's Ride," *Astronomy*, 20 (1992): 13–18.

27 Henry Wadsworth Longfellow. "Paul Revere's Ride" (1861). *The Complete Poetical Works of Henry Wadsworth Longfellow*, 1903.

CHAPTER TWO – MORE THAN TWO TAKE THE SHIP

1 David Wright, "Timeline for the Flood," Answers in Genesis, March 9, 2012, https://answersingenesis.org/bible-timeline/timeline-for-the-flood/.

2 James Strong, *The New Strong's Exhaustive Concordance of the Bible* (Nashville, TN: Thomas Nelson Publishers, 1990).

3 Ibid.

4 Jonathan Cahn, *The Book of Mysteries* (Lake Mary, FL: FrontLine, 2016), 104.

5 *The Chronological Study Bible* (Nashville, TN: Thomas Nelson Publishers, 2008), 14.

6 John Woodmorappe, *Noah's Ark: A Feasibility Study* (Dallas, TX: Institute for Creation Research, 2009).

7 Ibid.

8 Dimensions Info Editors, "Actual Size of Noah's Ark," DimensionsInfo, October 23, 2014, http://www.dimensionsinfo.com/actual-size-of-noahs-ark/.

9 Tim Chaffey, "Did Noah Bring Seven or Fourteen Clean Animals onto the Ark?" Answers in Genesis, February 1, 2019, https://answersingenesis.org/noahs-ark/did-noah-bring-fourteen-or-seven-animals/.

10 Charles C. Mann, *1491: New Revelations of the Americas Before Columbus* (New York: Vintage Books, 2006), 40.

11 The Editors of Encyclopaedia Britannica, "Iroquois Confederacy: American Indian Confederation," *Encyclopaedia Britannica*, retrieved May 13, 2020, https://www.britannica.com/topic/Iroquois-Confederacy#accordion-article-history.

12 Mann, *1491*, 119.

13   The Editors of Encyclopaedia Britannica, "Mohawk," *Encyclopaedia Britannica*, May 6, 2020, https://www.britannica.com/topic/Mohawk.

14   Mann, *1491*, 371.

15   Eldridge Henry Goss, *The Life of Colonel Paul Revere*, 2 vols. (Boston: Joseph George Cupples, 1891), 123–124.

CHAPTER THREE – THE SECRET OF A SUPPORTING ROLE

1   Frank Charles Thompson, *The Thompson Chain-Reference Bible*, 5th ed. (Indianapolis, IN: B. B. Kirkbride Bible Company, Inc., 1988), 33.

2   Genesis 27.

3   James Strong, *The New Strong's Exhaustive Concordance of the Bible* (Nashville, TN: Thomas Nelson Publishers, 1990).

4   Jerry Jones, *Cheated: What To Do When Life's Not Fair* (Hazelwood, MO: Word Aflame Press, 2007), 81–82, 85.

5   Strong, *The New Strong's Exhaustive Concordance*.

6   Jones, *Cheated*, 91.

7   Genesis 31:35.

8   Strong, *The New Strong's Exhaustive Concordance*, Hebrew ref. num. 1126, 22.

9   Genesis 49:30–31.

10   Strong, *The New Strong's Exhaustive Concordance*.

CHAPTER FOUR – EGYPT AND A DREAMER

1   Frank Charles Thompson, *The Thompson Chain-Reference Bible*, 5th ed. (Indianapolis, IN: B. B. Kirkbride Bible Company, Inc., 1988), 44–45.

2   Jonathan Cahn, *The Book of Mysteries* (Lake Mary, FL: FrontLine, 2016), 104.

3   James Strong, *The New Strong's Exhaustive Concordance of the Bible* (Nashville, TN: Thomas Nelson Publishers, 1990).

4   The Editors of Encyclopedia Britannica, "Intolerable Acts: Great Britain [1774]," *Encyclopedia Britannica*, January 15, 2019, https://www.britannica.com/event/Intolerable-Acts.

5   Editors, "Fairfax Resolves," Library of Congress, retrieved April 6, 2019, https://www.loc. gov/collections/george-washington-papers/articles-and-essays/fairfax-resolves/.

6   Samuel A. Forman, *Dr. Joseph Warren: The Boston Tea Party, Bunker Hill, and the Birth of American Liberty* (Gretna, LA: Pelican Publishing, 2012), 196.

7   John K. Alexander, *Samuel Adams: The Life of an American Revolutionary* (Lanham, MD: Rowman & Littlefield, 2011), 187–194.

8   Forman, *Dr. Joseph Warren*, 216.

9   National Park Service, "The Shot Heard Round the World," February 26, 2015, https://www.nps.gov/mima/learn/education/the-shot-heard-round-the-world.htm.

10 Forman, *Dr. Joseph Warren*, 104, 190.

11 Janet Uhlar, *Liberty's Martyr* (Indianapolis, IN: Dog Ear Publishing, 2009), 245.

12 Forman, *Dr. Joseph Warren*, 236.

13 Uhlar, *Liberty's Martyr*, 177.

14 Forman, *Dr. Joseph Warren*, 107.

15 Rudyard Kipling, "If," circa 1895, public domain, https://poets.org/poem/if.

16 Forman, *Dr. Joseph Warren*, 97.

17 Uhlar, *Liberty's Martyr*, 318.

18 Forman, *Dr. Joseph Warren*, 107.

19 Ibid.

20 Abraham Lincoln, "The Gettysburg Address," Speech, Gettysburg, PA, November 19, 1863, http://www.ushistory.org/documents/gettysburg.htm.

21 Description of "Tytler, Alexander Fraser, Lectures and Correspondence of Alexander Fraser Tytler, Lord Woodhouselee (1747–1813), 1798–1802. Edinburgh University Library Special Collections. GB 237 COLL-520" on the Archives Hub website, https://archiveshub.jisc.ac.uk /data/ gb237-coll-520.

22 Alexis de Tocqueville, *Democracy in America* (Harvey Mansfield and Delba Winthrop, trans., ed.: Chicago: University of Chicago Press, 2000).

23 Cal Thomas, *America's Expiration Date: The Fall of Empires and Superpowers … and the Future of the United States* (Grand Rapids, MI: Zondervan, 2020).

24 Alfred Edersheim, *Sketches of Jewish Social Life in the days of Christ* (Grand Rapids, MI: Wm. B. Eerdmans Publishing Company, 1976), 122.

1   Matthew 2:19–20.
2   John 1:14.
3   Kevin DeYoung, "Out of Egypt I Called My Son," The Gospel Coalition, December 9, 2010, https://www.thegospelcoalition.org/blogs/kevin-deyoung/3133.
4   1 Corinthians 15:21–22, 45–47.
5   1 Corinthians 10:2.
6   Luke 2:4.
7   Matthew 2:22a.
8   Matthew 2:22b–23.
9   Alfred Edersheim, *Sketches of Jewish Social Life in the days of Christ* (Grand Rapids, MI: Wm. B. Eerdmans Publishing Company, 1976), 44.
10 Edersheim, 136.
11 Matthew 13:55.
12 Matthew 3:16; Mark 1:10; Luke 3:22; John 1:32.
13 Charles Dickens, *A Tale of Two Cities* (London: Chapman & Hall, 1859).
14 History and Genealogy Reference Unit, "Colonial Records & Topics: The 1752 Calendar Change," Connecticut State Library, November 12, 2019, https://libguides.ctstatelibrary.org/hg/colonialresearch/calendar.
15 Ibid.
16 The Center for Legislative Archives, "George Washington's Birthday," The U.S. National Archives and Records Administration, June 19, 2019, https://www.archives.gov/legislative/ features/washington.
17 Independence Hall Association, "Carpenters' Hall," retrieved November 16, 2019, www.ushistory.org/tour/carpenters-hall.htm.
18 The Colonial Williamsburg Foundation, "The American Revolution: Patrick Henry (1736–1799)," retrieved November 23, 2019, http://www.ouramericanrevolution.org/index.cfm/ people/view/pp0004.
19 Peter Feuerherd, "The Strange History of Masons in America," JSTOR Daily, August 3, 2017, https://daily.jstor.org/the-strange-history-of-masons-in-america/.
20 Samuel A. Forman, *Dr. Joseph Warren: The Boston Tea Party, Bunker Hill, and the Birth of American Liberty* (Gretna, LA: Pelican Publishing, 2012), 63, 112.
21 Forman, *Dr. Joseph Warren*, 109–110.
22 Forman, 114.
23 Forman, 115.

24 Forman, 111–112.

25 Richard Frothingham, *Life and Times of Joseph Warren* (Whitefish, MT: Kessinger, 2007), 115.

26 Janet Uhlar, *Liberty's Martyr* (Indianapolis, IN: Dog Ear Publishing, 2009), 96.

27 Forman, *Dr. Joseph Warren*, 324.

28 Forman, 122.

CHAPTER SIX – SILVER AND A SALUTATION

1 *The Chronological Study Bible* (Nashville, TN: Thomas Nelson Publishers, 2008), 1215–1220, 1226.

2 David H. Stern, *Jewish New Testament Commentary* (Clarksville, MD: Jewish New Testament Publications, 1992), 38.

3 J. R. Dummelow, ed., *A Commentary on the Holy Bible* (New York: The Macmillan Company, 1961), 661.

4 Rev. Leslie F. Church, ed., *Commentary on the Whole Bible by Matthew Henry: Genesis to Revelation* (Grand Rapids, MI: Zondervan Publishing House, 1961), 1251.

5 Merrill C. Tenney, ed., *The Zondervan Pictorial Bible Dictionary* (Grand Rapids, MI: Zondervan Publishing House, 1963), 455–456.

6 Robert Wakefield, *Mayflower Families Through Five Generations* (vol. 18, part 2, 2nd ed.), (Plymouth, MA: General Society of Mayflower Descendants, 2011), 266–267.

7 Ibid.

8 Jill Lepore, *The Name of War: King Philip's War and the Origins of American Identity* (New York: Alfred A. Knopf, Inc.).

9 John Grenier, *The First Way of War: American War Making on the Frontier* (Cambridge, MA: Cambridge University Press, 2005), 35.

10 Robert S. Wakefield, *Richard Church and His Descendants for Four Generations* (Plymouth, MA: General Society of Mayflower Descendants, 1998), 119.

11 Samuel A. Forman, *Dr. Joseph Warren: The Boston Tea Party, Bunker Hill, and the Birth of American Liberty* (Gretna, LA: Pelican Publishing, 2012), 43.

12 Forman, 148.

13 Richard Frothingham, *Life and Times of Joseph Warren* (Whitefish, MT: Kessinger, 2007), 64–67.

14 United States History, "Benjamin Church," retrieved April 5, 2020, https://u-s-history.com/ pages/h1245.html.

15 Frothingham, *Life and Times of Joseph Warren*, 137.

16 Samuel A. Forman, "Naturally Impelled to Acts of Treachery: Benjamin Church's 1773 Boston Massacre Oration – Full Text," retrieved April 5, 2020, http://www.drjosephwarren.com/2013/04/naturally-impelled-to-acts-of-treachery-dr-church%e2%80%99s-1773-boston-massacre-oration-full-text/.

17 Forman, *Dr. Joseph Warren*, 194–195.

18 Forman, 166.

19 Forman, 167.

20 Frothingham, *Life and Times of Joseph Warren*, 206.

21 Frothingham, 207.

22 Forman, *Dr. Joseph Warren*, 167.

23 Forman, 159, 254.

24 Forman, 216, 222.

25 Janet Uhlar, *Liberty's Martyr* (Indianapolis, IN: Dog Ear Publishing, 2009), 194.

26 Ibid.

27 Uhlar, 246.

28 Forman, *Dr. Joseph Warren*, 276.

29 Forman, 273.

30 Uhlar, *Liberty's Martyr*, 247.

31 Allen French, *General Gage's Informers* (Ann Arbor: University of Michigan Press, 1932).

32 Ibid.

CHAPTER SEVEN – DEATH ON A HILL, LIFE IN THE TRENCHES

1 *The Chronological Study Bible* (Nashville, TN: Thomas Nelson Publishers, 2008), 1220, 1226, 1242, 1244.

2 Lee Strobel, *The Case for Christ: A Journalist's Personal Investigation of the Evidence for Jesus* (Grand Rapids, MI: Zondervan, 1998), 279.

3 Matthew 26:59, 66; 27:1; Mark 14:53, 55, 64; 15:1; Luke 23:1–2.

4 John 18:28.

5 Strobel, *The Case for Christ*, 283.

6 Kaari Ward, ed., *Jesus and His Times* (Pleasantville, NY: The Reader's Digest Association, Inc., 1987), 117.

7   Flavius Josephus, *Josephus: The Complete Works*, trans. William Whiston, A.M. (Nashville, TN: Thomas Nelson Publishers, 1998), 105.

8   Alisa Douer, *Egypt – The Lost Homeland: Exodus from Egypt, 1947-1967 – The History of the Jews in Egypt, 1540 BCE to 1967 CE* (Arabische Welt – Arab World: Logos Verlag, 2015), 277, footnote 190. ISBN 978-3832540524.

9   Gary William Poole, "Flavius Josephus: Jewish Priest, Scholar, and Historian," *Encyclopedia Britannica*, last modified January 3, 2020, https://www.britannica.com/biography/Flavius-Josephus

10 Ibid.

11 Steve Mason, ed., *Flavius Josephus: Translation and Commentary* (10 vols. in 12th ed.), (Leiden: BRILL, 2000), 12–13.

12 Harry Oates, "The Great Jewish Revolt of 66 CE," *Ancient History Encyclopedia*, last modified August 28, 2015, https://www.ancient.eu/article/823/.

13 Samuel A. Forman, *Dr. Joseph Warren: The Boston Tea Party, Bunker Hill, and the Birth of American Liberty* (Gretna, LA: Pelican Publishing, 2012), 190, 287.

14 Janet Uhlar, *Liberty's Martyr* (Indianapolis, IN: Dog Ear Publishing, 2009), 192, 236.

15 Uhlar, 274.

16 Forman, *Dr. Joseph Warren*, 294.

17 U.S. Army Center of Military History, "The U.S. Army: America's First National Institution," retrieved February 1, 2020, https://www.army.mil/1775/.

18 Richard Frothingham, *Life and Times of Joseph Warren* (Whitefish, MT: Kessinger, 2007), 511.

19 Uhlar, *Liberty's Martyr*, 238.

20 Forman, *Dr. Joseph Warren*, 222.

21 Forman, 295.

22 Forman, 254.

23 Forman, 286–287.

24 Board of Underwater Archeological Resources, "BUAR – Study on Battle of Chelsea Creek (1775)," retrieved February 8, 2020, https://www.mass.gov/service-details/buar-study-on-battle-of-chelsea-creek-1775.

25 Forman, *Dr. Joseph Warren*, 287.

26 Uhlar, *Liberty's Martyr*, 273.

27 Uhlar, 280.

28 Frothingham, *Life and Times of Joseph Warren*, 514.

29 Forman, *Dr. Joseph Warren*, 299.

30 Uhlar, *Liberty's Martyr*, 280.

31 Frothingham, *Life and Times of Joseph Warren*, 515.

32 Frothingham, 514.

33 Richard Frothingham, Jr., *History of the Siege of Boston and of the Battles of Lexington, Concord, and Bunker Hill, Second Edition* (Boston: Charles C. Little and James Brown, 1851), 194.

34 Todd Andrlik, "The 25 Deadliest Battles of the Revolutionary War," *Journal of the American Revolution*, May 13, 2014, https://allthingsliberty.com/2014/05/the-25-deadliest-battles-of-the-revolutionary-war/.

35 Uhlar, *Liberty's Martyr*, 228–229.

36 Uhlar, 297, 300.

37 Uhlar, back cover.

38 Forman, *Dr. Joseph Warren*, 306, 320.

39 Forman, 306, 317.

40 Uhlar, *Liberty's Martyr*, 299–305.

41 Uhlar, 301, 303.

42 Forman, *Dr. Joseph Warren*, 352.

43 Uhlar, *Liberty's Martyr*, 300.

44 Forman, *Dr. Joseph Warren*, 306.

45 Frothingham, *Life and Times of Joseph Warren*, 520.

46 Frothingham, 519.

47 Uhlar, *Liberty's Martyr*, 303.

48 Uhlar, 271, 300, 303.

49 Frothingham, *Life and Times of Joseph Warren*, 520.

50 Joseph J. Ellis, *Patriots: Brotherhood of the American Revolution* [Audio Book] (Recorded Books, LLC: Barnes & Noble Publishing, 2004), Disc 7.

51 Joseph Plumb Martin, *Narrative of a Revolutionary Soldier: Some of the Adventures, Dangers, and Sufferings of Joseph Plumb Martin* (New York: Signet Classics, 2001).

52 Joseph J. Ellis, *Patriots: Brotherhood of the American Revolution* [Course Syllabus] (Recorded Books, LLC: Barnes & Noble Publishing, 2004), 33.

53 Joseph J. Ellis, *Patriots: Brotherhood of the American Revolution* [Audio Book] (Recorded Books, LLC: Barnes & Noble Publishing, 2004), Disc 7.

54 Ibid.

55 Uhlar, *Liberty's Martyr*, 308.

56 Ellis, *Patriots* [Syllabus], 19.

57   Forman, *Dr. Joseph Warren*, 278.

58   Edward J. Cashin, "Revolutionary War in Georgia," *New Georgia Encyclopedia*, Georgia Humanities and the University of Georgia Press, last edited September 12, 2018, https://www.georgiaencyclopedia.org/articles/history-archaeology/revolutionary-war-georgia.

CHAPTER EIGHT – A RISING SUN AND A WAXING MOON

1   Richard Frothingham, *Life and Times of Joseph Warren* (Whitefish, MT: Kessinger, 2007), 522.

2   James Kirby Martin, *Benedict Arnold: Revolutionary Hero (An American Warrior Reconsidered)* (New York: University Press, 1997).

3   Samuel A. Forman, *Dr. Joseph Warren: The Boston Tea Party, Bunker Hill, and the Birth of American Liberty* (Gretna, LA: Pelican Publishing, 2012), 315–316.

4   Janet Uhlar, *Liberty's Martyr* (Indianapolis, IN: Dog Ear Publishing, 2009), 306.

5   Uhlar, 308–310.

6   Forman, *Dr. Joseph Warren*, 169, 178.

7   Forman, 317.

8   Uhlar, *Liberty's Martyr*, 309–310.

9   Frothingham, *Life and Times of Joseph Warren*, 522.

10 Frothingham, 524.

11 Forman, *Dr. Joseph Warren*, 317, 363.

12 Uhlar, *Dr. Joseph Warren*, 308.

13 Forman, *Dr. Joseph Warren*, 363.

14 Lindley S. Butler, *North Carolina and the Coming of the Revolution, 1763–1776* (Raleigh: North Carolina Department of Cultural Resources, Division of Archives and History, 1976).

15 Virginia Independence Bicentennial Commission. *Revolutionary Virginia: the Road to Independence, a Documentary Record, Vol 7: Independence and the Fifth Convention, 1776*. Compiled and edited by Robert L. Scribner and Brent Tarter (Charlottesville: University Press of Virginia, 1983).

16 *The Chronological Study Bible* (Nashville, TN: Thomas Nelson Publishers, 2008), 1249, 1252, 1256.

17 David H. Stern, *Jewish New Testament Commentary* (Clarksville, MD: Jewish New Testament Publications, 1992), 218.

18 Kenneth Barker, ed., *The NIV Study Bible* (Grand Rapids, MI: Zondervan Bible Publishers, 1985), 1645.

19   Charles John Ellicott, D.D., ed., *The Layman's Handy Commentary on the Bible: The Acts of the Apostles* (Grand Rapids, MI: Zondervan Publishing House, 1957), 34.

20   James Strong, *The New Strong's Exhaustive Concordance of the Bible* (Nashville, TN: Thomas Nelson Publishers, 1990).

21   Flavius Josephus, *Josephus: The Complete Works*, trans. William Whiston, A.M. (Nashville, TN: Thomas Nelson Publishers, 1998), 822.

22   Hugh Chisholm, ed., Entry for "Eleutheropolis," *1911 Encyclopedia Britannica* (1910), https://www.studylight.org/encyclopedias/bri/e/eleutheropolis.html.

23   David S. Potter, *The Roman Empire at Bay, AD 180–395* (New York: Routledge, 2004).

24   CartaJerusalem: The Hub for Biblical Geography & History, "Bet Guvrin (Betogabris)," retrieved April 29, 2020, http://carta-jerusalem.com/biblical-sites/bet-guvrin-betogabris/.

25   Clinton Rossiter, *1787: The Grand Convention* (New York: W.W. Norton, 1987).

26   Oak Hill Publishing, "Fascinating Facts about the U.S. Constitution," retrieved April 29, 2020, https://www.constitutionfacts.com/us-constitution-amendments/fascinating-facts/.

27   Jonathan Cahn, *The Book of Mysteries* (Lake Mary, FL: FrontLine, 2016), 52.

28   John R. Vile, ed., "Rising Sun" in *The Constitutional Convention of 1787: A Comprehensive Encyclopedia of America's Founding*, Vol. 1 (Santa Barbara, CA: ABC-CLIO, 2005), 681.

EPILOGUE

1   Richard Frothingham, *Life and Times of Joseph Warren* (Whitefish, MT: Kessinger, 2007), 396, 485, 487.

2   Frothingham, 507.

3   Samuel A. Forman, *Dr. Joseph Warren: The Boston Tea Party, Bunker Hill, and the Birth of American Liberty* (Gretna, LA: Pelican Publishing, 2012), 324.

4   Forman, 368–369.

5   Forman, 327.

6   Forman, 163.

7   Forman, 328.

8   Andy Andrews, *The Butterfly Effect: How Your Life Matters* (Naperville, IL: Simple Truths, LLC, 2009).

9   Samuel A. Forman, "Ronald Reagan Inspired by Joseph Warren," *YouTube*, October 20, 2011, https://www.youtube.com/watch?v=HK8nT2P387w.

10 Ibid, 1:15.

11 Samuel A. Forman, *Dr. Joseph Warren*, 334.

ABOUT THE AUTHOR

Philip Strouse has spent the majority of his life in public service and has received several awards for bridging gaps and building partnerships. He earned a master's degree in emergency and disaster management from American Military University and a Bachelor of Science with military distinction from the U.S. Air Force Academy. He lives with his wife, Donna, and two sons, Kaleb and Keaton, in Newnan, Georgia.

Lightning Source UK Ltd.
Milton Keynes UK
UKHW041446101120
373146UK00008B/515/J